MAN AND MISSION

E. B. Gaston and the Origins of the Fairhope Single Tax Colony

Paul M. Gaston

The Black Belt Press

Montgomery

The Black Belt Press
P.O. Box 551
Montgomery, AL 36101

Design by Randall Williams

Manufactured in the United States of America.

Library Of Congress Cataloging-In-Publication Data
Gaston, Paul M., 1928-.
        Man and Mission: E.B. Gaston and the Origins of
the Fairhope Single Tax Colony/ by Paul M. Gaston
                p.   cm.
Includes bibliographical references (p.   ) and index
        ISBN 1-881320-10-3

1. Fairhope Single Tax Corporation — History. 2. Utopian
socialism — Alabama —Fairhope —History. Gaston,
Ernest B. 4. Socialists — United States — Biography. 5.
Fairhope (Ala.) — History. I. Title.
HX656.F35G37   1993
335'.976121 — dc20   93-7774
                                          CIP

To my cousins,

the surviving grandchildren of
ERNEST AND CLARA GASTON:

Olive Jean Gaston Woodward

James Ernest Gaston, Jr.

Mary Frances Gaston Godard

Max Pittinger McGill, Jr.

Clara Louise Gaston Wengert

Mary Edith McGill Green

Frances Harriette McGill Jernigan

We shall not cease from exploration
And the end of all our exploring
Will be to arrive where we started
And know the place for the first time.
—T. S. Eliot[1]

Utopia has long been another name for the unreal and the impossible. We have set utopia over against the world. As a matter of fact, it is our utopias that make the world tolerable to us: the cities and mansions that people dream of are those in which they finally live. The more that men react upon their environment and make it over after a human pattern, the more continuously do they live in utopia; but when there is a breach between the world of affairs and the overworld of utopia, we become conscious of the part that the will-to-utopia has played in our lives, and we see our utopia as a separate reality.
—Lewis Mumford[2]

They that shall make good theories work and prove the value of proposed social solutions by practical demonstration will do far more to move the world than the wisest and most brilliant theorists.
—E. B. Gaston[3]

All references are given in Notes, beginning on page 120.

Contents

E.B. Gaston in 1894, the year he led settlers to Alabama.

Preface

THIS IS A BOOK ABOUT A MAN, ERNEST B. GASTON, and a mission, the creation of the Fairhope Single Tax Colony. I briefly characterize Fairhope's history over the past century in the first chapter. The remaining seven chapters describe Gaston's intellectual journey in the 1880s and 1890s and the ways in which he and his colleagues hoped to engage the difficult social and economic issues of their age by creating a model community. The book ends as Fairhope begins.

E. B. Gaston was my grandfather. I was not quite ten when he died, and my memory of him is dim, but I always understood his special relationship to Fairhope. I came to imbibe the values of the community as I grew up in it, and to understand it as only an insider can. I have tried to use that special knowledge in writing this book, but I have also tried to guard against its potentially warping effect by seeking the distance and discipline of a professional historian.

That task is made easier by the wealth of material in the archives of the Fairhope Single Tax Corporation. In addition to the official records of the colony, all well preserved, I found there extensive correspondence to and from my grandfather, as well as the complete files of the *Fairhope Courier*. Unless I note otherwise, all of the primary material I cite in the notes is in the colony archives.

I began systematic work on the history of Fairhope more than fifteen years ago. Several short publications have appeared since then, but not the comprehensive history I hope one day to complete.[4] When that book appears I will thank the many persons who have helped me over the years. Here I want to acknowledge those who have made this small volume possible.

In March of 1992 I asked Randall Williams if he would print a sixty-page pamphlet for me on the origins of Fairhope. I was taken aback when he said no. After all, he was supposed to be a friend. When he added that he would publish a short book on the subject a great cloud lifted. His encouragement and enthusiasm never wavered and I owe the existence of the book to this gifted editor. I am proud to be published under his imprint.

I presented the first draft of the manuscript to my colleagues in the History Department Workshop at the University of Virginia in September of 1992. The reception was heartening and the suggestions for improvement wonderfully varied and helpful. For their presence and encouragement I thank Ed Ayers; Brian Balogh; Alice Carter; Bob Cross; Rebecca Edwards; Megan Holden; Michael Holt; Ann Lane; Juliette Landphair; Mel Leffler; Andy Lewis; Nelson Lichtenstein; Brad Mittendorf; Duane Osheim; Anne Rubin; Pat Sullivan; and David Throup. Bill Taylor and Ann Schutte also gave me very helpful suggestions.

Lisa Szefel helped as my research assistant and showed me what an accomplished editor she is. Gwyneth Love, director of the Oberlin in London program, made me the beneficiary of her acute sense of style and tone to point me to many needed improvements. Gale Rowe, secretary of the Fairhope Single Tax Corporation, supported me all the way, gave me guidance on critical points, and generously shared his reactions with me. Fairhope is lucky to have him.

Fitz Brundage, of Queen's University, Kingston, Canada, kindly let me read his unpublished essay on "The Utopian Moment in the New South." He also shared with me his knowledge of the Ruskin colony and commented helpfully on my Fairhope work. Ron Yanosky found time during his first year of teaching at Harvard to read the manuscript and guide me to a better understanding of the national single-tax movement, the subject of his dissertation. He sent me numerous detailed suggestions—all of them immensely helpful—gave me a copy of his unpublished paper, "The Colored Farmers' Alliance and the Single Tax," and granted me permission to quote parts of it and to cite some of his other unpublished findings. This is scholarly generosity at its best, and I am deeply grateful for it.

My daughter, Chinta Gaston, pronounced the book good, and then marked up all but a few of my pages with red ink. She spotted sloppy constructions, suggested felicitous alternatives, and made me aware of ambiguous arguments and unwarranted expectations of my readers. I hope she will be available for the next book. Bill Abbot, my colleague and neighbor, has never ceased urging me to get on with my Fairhope work. He read this installment, pointing out dozens of ways to give it greater precision, clarity, and subtlety. I am fortunate to be among those who have been nurtured by his caring and by his sensitivity to our language.

Mary Gaston has been involved in every stage of my study of Fairhope's history. She understands its nuances and is always there to share her insights with me. I have depended on her editing, as always, from first rough paragraph to last polished draft. Finally, although he was not here to read this manuscript, my father, the late Cornie Gaston, was a constant presence as I wrote it. He told me much that I could have learned nowhere else and his measured judgments were always bench mark reminders.

PAUL M. GASTON
Charlottesville, Virginia
January 15, 1993

MAN AND MISSION

I

Looking Backward, 1994-1894

A PARTY OF TWENTY-EIGHT SETTLERS—NINETEEN adults and nine children—arrived on the eastern shore of Mobile Bay in November of 1894. Strangers to the land, and mostly to each other, they were driven by idealism and armed with a blueprint for a better world. Their purpose, as their freshly drawn constitution put it, was "to establish and conduct a model community or colony, free from all forms of private monopoly" so that they might enjoy "equality of opportunity, the full reward of individual efforts, and the benefits of co-operation in matters of general concern." They came hoping for a better life for themselves. But they also hoped that their model community might show others how the "unnatural and unjust" conditions under which they believed Americans were forced to live might be removed. The economic system of the United States, ravaged by monopoly capitalism, violated the "natural rights" of its citizens, was "at war with the nobler impulses of humanity, and opposed to its highest development." All of that could be changed by "intelligent association" dedicated to revealing a better way to organize and conduct human activity.[5]

With a fair hope for the success of their venture, these ambitious reformers called themselves Fairhopers and chose the name Fairhope for the community they would establish.

Americans today, like citizens everywhere in the industrialized democracies of the world, are likely to find something quaintly irrelevant in the spectacle of a tiny band of ordinary individuals, alone on a sparsely settled seashore, speaking of conquering the "unnatural and unjust" conditions of their society in order to free the "nobler impulses of humanity" to reach its "highest development." Accustomed to thinking of social changes coming from great impersonal forces or from the power of surging mass movements, we of the 1990s cannot imagine marching to the beat of the utopian impulse. How could such a journey today possibly banish poverty, eliminate injustice, and foster more humane relationships in our vast, complex, and interdependent world?

We are not the first to think this way. A hundred years ago most Americans said much the same thing. Among the skeptics were some of the most influential apostles of social change. Henry George and Edward Bellamy, the two most famous, warned against trying to reform the society with experimental, demonstration communities. They feared that the smallness and isolation of such efforts would cause them to fail, thereby discrediting the very theories they championed. But in those days not everyone heeded their warnings. Thousands of hopeful reformers from all parts of the country, and Europe as well, became communitarian reformers. They set out to change the world by creating model communities to show the virtues of their utopian ideals. Most of these efforts failed; many lasted for only a few years, if that, but new ones kept arising.

This late nineteenth century communitarian impulse does not resonate with most of us of the late twentieth century; but, if we let

4

ourselves penetrate the unfamiliar language and discussions of public policy issues of that time, we should be overwhelmed with the familiarity of descriptions of a society in crisis. Henry George's statement that the great progress of his age brought with it unprecedented poverty is echoed in the assertions of our own time that the rich have become richer, the poor have become poorer, and that a greater proportion of our people have fallen into poverty than in any other major industrial country. The descriptions of social unrest and urban squalor from those days resemble the accounts of deprivation, homelessness, and ghetto explosions of our own times. The Populist Party lament of 1892 that the nation was on the verge of "moral, political, and material ruin" is heard again in the chilling 1992 essay of economist Ray Marshall. He tells us that "inequality as extreme as ours destroys democratic institutions" and he fears that we may "now rank last among the industrialized democracies of the world in achieving, as a whole, the goals of a democratic society."[6]

We have good reasons to look at the complex world of a century ago. Reminders of unsettling paradox and enduring injustice are not pleasant, but we may also find hope and guidance in the vision, courage, and tenacity of men and women who gave that era an all-but-forgotten richness and distinction. The story of Fairhope's origins is a small part of the history of the search for a more just and humane world. But it is a part. Touched in one way or another by nearly all of the ferment of the late 1880s and early 1890s, Fairhope's architects sifted through a dazzling variety of ideas, movements, and organizations to clarify their vision of what a better world might be and how it could be created. To watch the unfolding of that odyssey is to enter deeply into one of the enduring aspects of the American experience.

It is also to examine another of the enduring aspects of the American experience—the ways in which a single individual may make a difference in the historical process. Several hands were involved in the making of Fairhope, but without Ernest B. Gaston it would not have existed. A young Iowa newspaper man and reformer, Gaston worked out the unique theories that became the colony plan. It was also he who organized the movement to recruit settlers and led them in November of 1894 to their promised land. The story of Fairhope's origins is the story of both a man and his mission.

Fairhope will celebrate its centenary in 1994. No other American community established to demonstrate a secular reform philosophy has even approached this record of longevity.[7] Fairhope's claim to that achievement, however, must be qualified. A cooperative community advocating Henry George's single-tax program to make land common property, the Fairhope colony was founded in 1894. It was called the Fairhope Industrial Association. Ten years later it changed its name to the Fairhope Single Tax Corporation. In 1908 the colony's independent status was lost when the town of Fairhope was incorporated. The colony then became part of the town in a complicated arrangement that still puzzles strangers. Since 1908, when the municipality was created, there have been two Fairhopes; or, perhaps to put it better, the town of Fairhope has contained two major elements—the "colony" people, living on single-tax colony land and taking part in the demonstration of the Georgist principles, and the non-colony people, living on privately-owned land and having no formal relationship and no commitment to the single-tax colony.

Fairhope is today a charming city of nearly nine thousand persons, growing rapidly in a rapidly growing area of coastal Alabama. The Fairhope Single Tax Corporation owns about 30 percent of the land within the city limits (including the main business district) and some 2,300 acres of land in unincorporated parts of the county. Its declared purpose continues to be to demonstrate the virtues of George's philosophy; with only minor alterations, the constitution the founders brought with them in 1894 remains in effect.

Over the last few decades the generally conventional values and policies of the municipality have come to dominate Fairhope. The community's sense of identity is influenced in many ways by its utopian heritage, and most people who live there are proud of their city's fame and unique history. But Fairhope as a town can no longer be defined by the utopian ideals of its pioneer settlers almost a century ago. This outcome was predicted by an area newspaper writer long ago. Reflecting in 1908 on the likely consequences of municipalization, he said, "Fairhope will be known hereafter as a town, and the name 'colony' will go out of use, except to describe certain local usages, such as 'colony rents' and 'colony lands.'"[8] But that prophecy badly misjudged the depth and tenacity of the colony idea. Fairhope's fame, in fact, continued to spread after 1908 and for many years it was widely known as the home of the single-tax colony, a unique community distinguished by its radical ideas and institutions, as well as its creative and colorful personalities.

One Fairhoper wrote early in the century of the special bonds of community that attracted reformers to it and sustained it as a lively intellectual and cultural center. There was a "spirit of comradeship" there that she had not experienced elsewhere. It gave meaning to life and direction to one's actions. Another early colonist rejected beautiful surroundings and material advantages as primary reasons for living in Fairhope. "Fairhope has an ideal," he wrote; commitment to that ideal was the source of Fairhope's real attraction.[9] Born of the colonists' quest for a humane, egalitarian society, the "spirit of comradeship" rooted in service to an ideal flourished long after the town was formed, reaching its apogee in the 1920s.

By that time evidence of the experiment's success had many faces. The colony's land policy attracted industrious settlers of modest means. Nowhere else could they acquire home, farm, and business sites without cost, being required only to pay into the common treasury an annual rental based on the land's value. The natural beauty of the location was enhanced by cooperative development of the woodlands, ravines, and bay front—and was protected from private monopoly by a public policy that declared scarce resources to belong to all citizens. These policies nurtured a kind of democratic communalism. Few people were either rich or poor; hierarchy and pretension found unfertile soil; social intercourse was easy and informal; homes were simple but often innovative and appealing; architecture and town development reflected a society free of sharp class divisions.

The colony's policies of free land, public improvements, community-owned utilities, and open park lands benefited colonists and non-colonists alike. Industrious working people of modest means formed the backbone of the town of Fairhope. But writers, actors, artists, and craftsmen also found the atmosphere congenial and initiated an enduring commitment to creative expression. A sprinkling of famous visitors—among them Upton Sinclair, Sherwood Anderson, Charless Ingersoll, Mrs. Henry Ford, Elizabeth Mead, Harold Ickes, Wharton

Esherick, and Clarence Darrow—enriched the intellectual and cultural life of the community and fostered a cosmopolitan atmosphere. Not surprisingly, the community also had more than its share of mavericks, people who expressed strong opinions on how life ought to be lived, what was most healthful to eat, what forms of dress (or undress) were most natural, and how individuals ought to relate to one another and to their environment.

In 1907 a Minnesota school teacher named Marietta Johnson, drawn to Fairhope by its reformist philosophy, founded the School of Organic Education. She directed her school for three decades, became a leader of the national progressive education movement, and turned what she called the "Fairhope Idea in Education" into a modest national force. School and colony meshed to add dynamism and an expanded mission to the community. A follower of John Dewey, America's leading philosopher of progressive education, Johnson argued that children reared on the competitive ethic of the American school system were unlikely to grow up to be the cooperative, reform-minded, justice-oriented citizens Fairhope wished to produce. The single tax alone was not enough, she said; it needed an educational foundation. With enthusiastic colony support, her school worked to provide that foundation. Dewey himself came to visit in 1913 and liked what he saw: a demonstration of "how the ideal of equality of opportunity for all is to be transmuted into reality."[10]

Fairhopers believed that their model community, imperfect though it was, gave the nation an example to follow. But even at the height of its fame in the 1920s there were few signs of progress toward converting others and no program to accomplish that goal. The municipality itself made no effort to adopt the single-tax system and neighboring communities were similarly unmoved by the widespread recognition of Fairhope's growth and popularity. The many favorable reports written about it inspired interest and admiration, but not emulation.

The Great Depression of the 1930s and the World War that followed were watershed years in Fairhope's history. The depression years were a time of diminished funds, shrinking outside interest in both the colony and the school, and the passing of the old leadership. E. B. Gaston died in 1937, Marietta Johnson a year later. A new generation of leaders, many of them children of the pioneer families, kept the colony and the school functioning, but neither of these institutions would ever again be the dominant influence in the town it had once been.[11] With the coming of the war, shipbuilding, an air force base, and other war-related activities in nearby Mobile drew thousands of workers to south Alabama, and Fairhope's population nearly doubled. This demographic revolution, started by wartime conditions, continued in the post-war years, and increasing numbers of men and women employed in Mobile made their homes on the eastern shore. Few of the newcomers were Fairhopers, understanding or sharing the sense of purpose that had earlier defined the town.[12]

Fairhope ceased to be mentioned in discussions of radical or utopian movements and was no longer a magnet for people looking to solve social problems. Instead, it took on more of the characteristics of southern small-town life, including the defense of segregation and the support of George Wallace during the civil rights era. After the Wallace era its politics turned increasingly conservative Republican.[13] In the early 1970s it was featured as the only Alabama town in a book called *Safe Places East*, a guide for Americans who wanted to escape—not solve—social problems, and it now shows up regularly in lists of safe harbors for the golden years.[14] A visiting *New Yorker* writer at the end of the 1970s, lamenting the passing of the old spirit of communitarian reform and the emergence of a new ethos, said that the people who lived in Fairhope seemed just like any other Americans.[15]

Such a facile observation highlights the ironies of Fairhope's history, but misses entirely the contemporary complexity of its character. The single taxers may no longer set the tone of the community or dominate public policy decisions, but they continue to be influential. And, for the first time in years, membership is growing and the members are vigorously debating ways of revitalizing their demonstration and spreading knowledge of their single-tax philosophy. It may also be true that the dominant social thought of the town tilts rightward, but no other small southern city, apart from a handful of university seats, fosters such a wide variety of ideologies, or as much lively intellectual discussion, artistic expression, and literary and theatrical creativity.

The powerful influence of the colony heritage is evident in these and other facets of contemporary Fairhope. Nowhere, however, is it more apparent than in the continuing demonstration of the founders' determination that scarce community resources should never be privately owned or developed for private gain. As the coastal areas along Mobile Bay and the Gulf of Mexico have fallen under the relentless assault of land speculators and developers, Fairhope stands more strikingly than ever before as an oasis, a tiny spot preserved from surrounding offenses and barriers to the people. Its celebrated park lands along the bluffs and the beaches below give vistas that cannot be closed—all because of the founding philosophy that land should be common property.

Ironically, Fairhope's very success in attracting a steadily increasing flow of new inhabitants now threatens its future. There is no more unoccupied colony land to take up, and the demand for deeded land puts it out of the price range of persons of modest means who once would have found their futures on free colony land. Whether Fairhope can withstand these demographic pressures into the next century is an open question. They seem almost certain to intensify rather than ameliorate class divisions and to subvert rather than nurture bonds of community. This may therefore be a good time to inquire into Fairhope's origins—to ask why and how it was created, and to consider afresh the solutions its founders offered to the universal and enduring problems of human community.

II

A Call to Action

A DOZEN IOWA REFORMERS ANSWERED ERNEST B. Gaston's call to come to his Des Moines office on January 4, 1894, to hear a paper he had written and to listen to a proposal he wished to make. It was the winter of a great depression and reports of human suffering and economic calamity came from all parts of the nation. Gaston's twelve friends, well known to each other and to their young host, were seasoned critics of their country, Jeremiahs gifted at condemning the plundering spirit of the age in which they lived. They surely nodded in agreement that day when Gaston spoke of the "enormous waste of human energy and natural resources" and the "hideous injustice and cruelty" which he saw woven more tightly each day into the fabric of American life. Opportunities for honest men were vanishing, he told them, "as one industry after another goes into the hands of trusts and the broad acres of our common heritage pass under the control of speculators." In the fiercely individualistic, competitive world that America was becoming, he believed, material success was possible only for those who would sacrifice their sense of justice and anesthetize their concern for their fellow human beings.[16]

Gaston and his friends were political warriors in a common

crusade. For three years they had been hopeful workers in the cause of the new Populist Party—grandly called "The People's Party"—drawn to it out of many reform activities and organizations in which they had trained. Their gathering place, where they met regularly to talk over ideas and strategies, was the office of the *Farmer's Tribune*, a long-time journal of dissent and now the voice of Iowa Populism. Their animated conversations around the stove became angry broadsides in their newspaper. "Thousands of people are starving and freezing," it announced just a few weeks after Gaston's meeting with his comrades. One outrage after another was recorded: "soup houses and police hall corridors . . . are everywhere thronged by thousands of the victims of the most damnable financial policy that ever disgraced a civilized nation," all in a country "filled with grain, fruit and all of labor's products," yet where "the laborers go into paupers' and felons' graves."[17] Presiding over many of these conversations was General James B. Weaver, the paper's editor and the Party's 1892 presidential candidate. Gaston joined the editorial staff in 1891; the next year, as managing editor, he freed Weaver to travel the country campaigning for the presidency.

The deepening depression and spreading misery were not the only sources of the despair felt by the once optimistic reformers. Inspired by the vision and caught up in the enthusiasm of the Populist revolt they were saddened by the country's rejection of the humane alternative they believed they had offered it. The Populist Party campaign of 1892 produced memorable rhetoric and enduring inspiration, but the electoral impact was slight. In Iowa, where Weaver won less than 5 percent of the vote, the outcome was especially discouraging. After the 1893 state and local elections, which likewise provided no encouragement, Gaston decided he had had enough of electoral politics. He reached the "disagreeable conclusion," as he was to put it later, "that the road to the achievement of the reforms necessary to establish justice in the country at large, was a long and tedious one, the end of which might not be reached in time to do him individually any good." Some other way must be found; some other outlet for reformist vision and energy must be hit upon.[18]

It was at this point that Gaston called on his twelve friends to listen to him read the paper he had been struggling to perfect for the past several months. He entitled it "True Co-operative Individualism," and at its conclusion he asked his comrades to "consider plans for the organization of a cooperative Colony or Community." His question for them was a challenging one: would they join him in building, somewhere on American virgin land, an alternative society in which they might plant and nurture the ingredients of a model social order? By creating their own community, he argued, they could offer to the country a visible example of a better way of life and perhaps in this way find the base and the leverage for reform that the political process seemed to deny them. At the same time they could provide almost immediately a satisfying environment for themselves, free from the corrupting moral and material imperatives of the larger society.

The young crusader was apparently persuasive. Acting as secretary of the meeting he had called, Gaston recorded, in the minute book in which he wrote for the first time that day, that the group voted "to prepare a draft constitution and bye laws and articles of incorporation and suggest plans for putting the ideas into practical operation at once."[19]

The man who inspired such enthusiasm among his friends had just passed his thirty-second birthday. Born in Henderson, Knox County,

James Estep Gaston, father of E.B. Gaston.

Illinois, on November 21, 1861, Ernest Berry Gaston probably thought little about his lineage, but enterprising genealogists can trace it back at least to a rebellious noble ancestor named Jean Gaston de Foix, a French Huguenot born in 1600. Presumably guaranteed religious toleration by the Edict of Nantes, French Protestants like Jean Gaston found the reality sadly different. Long before Louis XIV formally revoked the edict in 1685, perhaps in the 1640s, Jean appears to have been banished and to have fled to Scotland in search of a more congenial religious climate. His sons, discomfited in turn by religious discrimination in Scotland, migrated in the 1660s to County Antrim, Ireland. From Ireland a number of Gastons eventually made their way to the American colonies, some to South Carolina, some to New Jersey and Pennsylvania, and some to New England. One of these was a Hugh Gaston, born in Ireland in 1687. He sailed for the colonies early in the eighteenth century and his son, William, was the first of Hugh's American-born sons. William's son, John, helped to win independence for the colonies, serving as a major in the Northampton County militia of Pennsylvania. The Pennsylvania Gastons were a prolific clan. John and his wife Charity Cheeseman had eight children. One of those, James, married Mary Estep and they had nine children, the eighth of whom was E. B. Gaston's father, James Estep Gaston, born in 1809.[20]

By the time he married Sarah Kirk in 1838, James Estep Gaston had left the Baptist Church of his youth to follow Alexander Campbell into the newly revived Church of Christ where he became a zealous minister. Tutored by the famous Campbell and later joining him on tours through the midwest he was described by his mentor as "one of our best preachers," a man "distinguished for good sense, good talent and unfeigned piety." He had virtually no formal schooling, but he was admired as a student of Latin and Greek and hailed as both a good writer and compelling orator. He also carried on in the prolific tradition of his forebears. Sarah gave birth to six children before she died in 1853. The next year James married Catherine Estep Atkinson, a widowed cousin with two daughters of her own. James and Catherine had four additional children over the next seven years. The last of these was Ernest Berry Gaston. The family lived on a farm while the father ministered to his town congregation in Henderson. Despite his many siblings and half-siblings, Ernest grew up in a small household. Four of his brothers and sisters died before he was born, two died while he was a child, and four of the five who lived to his maturity set up on their own early in his life. Only his half-sister Clara was an enduringly important figure to him.[21]

James Gaston's preaching had taken him to pastorates in Illinois, Ohio, and Iowa. Early in 1864 he received a call to the newly-formed Central Church of Des Moines, the first Christian church established in the city. He had a successful ministry for three years until ill health forced his early retirement. Improved health later allowed him to take up pastorates for brief periods in other Iowa cities as well as in Kansas, but a lingering illness, apparently punctuated by bouts of depression, brought him back to Des Moines, where he lived in retirement until his death in 1888.[22]

Ernest Gaston grew up in the midwestern villages and towns where his father's preaching took the family. Settled in Des Moines before he was very far along in school, he came to maturity there. Scraps of evidence suggest that he was a restless youth whose behavior was less than exemplary, especially for a minister's son. "I readily acquired and easily held the reputation of being one of the worst boys in school," he recalled in an 1887 speech, "and achieved the high honor of being suspended three times in a little more than a month, to say nothing of the minor punishments which were almost of daily occurrence." Accompanying his rebellious spirit was a wide-ranging curiosity along with energy and intellect to pursue it. "I longed for a change," he confessed in the 1887 speech, apparently referring to his personal situation but perhaps seeing that linked to some larger social cause. In any case, he had not found what he wished for; he was "still longing for change." He wrote fondly of his adventure as a tenderfoot on a Texas cattle buying trip, but the life of a cowboy held no real appeal. At twenty-one, he entered Drake University, in the Des Moines suburb of University Place. His student career was interrupted by periods of employment in Minnesota and Kansas, the student magazine describing him once as "a business man of Minneapolis."[23] He graduated from the commerce department at the top of his class in 1886, at the age of twenty-four.[24]

College years were fruitful for Gaston. He worked hard, learned to write effectively, and became a popular orator. A speaker with a commanding presence, he was also a gifted singer, with a rich bass voice. His singing performances, usually as part of a quartet, became familiar campus entertainment. Some time in the winter of 1885-86 he met Clara Mershon. A recent arrival from Jones County, Iowa, Clara was a music student, and she and Ernest were members of the same student literary and musical society. They were married on November 24, 1887, just after Ernest had turned twenty-six and a month before her twenty-fifth birthday. Her family had recently moved to Des Moines from Jones County, and by the time of the marriage her father and brothers were gaining prominence with their merchandising store.[25]

At twenty-six, E. B. Gaston was well known around University Place for his zest and his imaginative enterprises. As a student he had won praise for his one-horse snow plow that kept the sidewalks free of snow. In the fall of 1886 he was elected justice of the peace. Not long after his election the student magazine reported that "Squire Gaston" was "making a vigorous warfare against the violation of the prohibition law in the city." Elected to a second term as justice of the peace, Gaston honed his political skills by holding other public offices. Between 1886-1890 he served as town recorder, City Council member, and fire chief of University Place.[26] In the business world, he acquired and operated a livery stable. The stable was soon abandoned when he put his business and building skills to work as a real estate developer. He bought several lots in University Place, built homes on them, and confidently looked forward to making a profit—not only from his labor and capital investment but also from the rise in land values anticipated in that growing section of Des Moines.

In the fall of 1889 Gaston marked his twenty-eighth birthday and he and Clara celebrated the second anniversary of their marriage. Unusual energy, ambition, and imagination had brought the young Gaston a measure of financial security and the respect of his fellow citizens in University Place as well. He had excelled as a student, held a variety of public offices, shown shrewd judgment as an enterprising businessman, and now was doing well in real estate. He was popular with the university set, in frequent demand as toastmaster, singer, and orator. Notices of "ice cream socials" usually featured a performance of one sort or another by him. He had a passion for horse races and seems to have enjoyed life. From all accounts his marriage to Clara was a happy one. The arrival of their first child in January, 1889, was both satisfying and a mark of their well being. Now, in the fall of 1889, a second was on the way. One might have envisioned for the future Gaston and his wife fitting comfortably into the life of their community, rearing a large family and expanding their circle of friends while Ernest enlarged his business activities and assumed the many tasks of civic leadership that seemed to await him.[27]

Instead, the restless spirit that was a family trademark took a new turn in him. Perhaps the death of his father the previous year was a catalyst. In any case, just as he was on the verge of entering a stable and conventional pattern of life he veered in new directions. He began by abruptly abandoning the one occupation that seemed sure to give him material security, denouncing real estate development as "speculative building," and proclaiming: "I want no more of it." At twenty-eight his developing social conscience made him find something immoral in a quintessentially American way of earning a living and sent him searching for ways to release the reformist drive that increasingly seemed to be giving direction to his life.[28]

III

A Reformer's World

THE AMERICA OF GASTON'S YOUNG MANHOOD WAS changing rapidly, and not in ways that made him proud of his country. Even the most casual inquiries turned up gruesome tales of deepening poverty, wrenching class conflict, with violent confrontations between industrial workers and factory owners. Many young intellectuals, the historian Dorothy Ross writes, believed they were living in an age of "profound historical crisis," in which cherished republican values were being threatened by the new industrial capitalism. "Unadulterated capitalism," according to another authority, seemed to many to be on the verge of destroying the social order. Richard T. Ely, one of the young scholars of that era, believed that the workings of the new system of competitive individualism were "as cruel as laws of nature." He declared that "our food, our clothing, our shelter, all our wealth, is covered with stains and clots of blood." As Ross observes, many of the intellectuals who etched these searing indictments were "nurtured in evangelical piety, Whiggish moral politics, and the Christian ethicism of the American colleges," a trio of influences that had been working on Gaston; and, like the better-known critics whom Ross describes, Gaston was increasingly drawn to the "organic and idealistic thrust of socialism" in his search for answers to the social riddle. "Capital is allowed to control all *opportunity*," he wrote about this time, "and give the laborers only enough of their product to keep their souls and bodies together."[29]

Passionate and eager to find answers, Gaston embarked on an extraordinary five-year intellectual and moral odyssey that culminated in the founding of the model community he would call Fairhope.

He began his journey in August of 1889 by purchasing the two-year-old *Suburban Advocate*, a small newspaper serving University Place. News analysis and editorial writing were better suited to Gaston's temperament than land speculation. Journalism was also more congenial to his new passion for the study of American society, for seeking answers to the problems it created, and, especially, for finding an appropriate role for himself. A college classmate wrote approvingly from Colorado of the paper, remarking that "we can see ever so much of Ernest in it"; a friend from Minneapolis expressed his "trust" in the "citizenship" guidance he found in Gaston's writings.[30] Unfortunately, no copies of the *Advocate* have survived; other evidence, however, indicates that editing it gave Gaston the opportunity to explore new ideas, develop his persuasive powers, and extend his sphere of influence.

Gaston took a second fateful step in the autumn of 1889. He brought together a small group of friends—one was a former Drake professor and another his father-in-law—to form what they called the Des Moines Investigating Club—a club to "investigate" the social and economic condition of the United States by bringing the members abreast of the best and latest literature. Gaston looked on the club as a forum for gaining perspective, broadening and testing his ideas, and sharpening his editorial skills. The group met weekly throughout the winter, discussing such popular works of social criticism as Edward Bellamy's *Looking Backward*, Henry George's *Progress and Poverty*, and Laurence Gronlund's *The Cooperative Commonwealth*.[31]

Gaston did nothing new when he established the Investigating Club. All across the country in the summer and fall of 1889 similar groups were being formed, most of them to champion the social theories of Edward Bellamy. Bellamy's utopian novel, *Looking Backward*, appeared at the beginning of 1888 and in the next year the enthusiasm it generated led to the creation of a magazine, the *Nationalist*, and a network of clubs claiming six thousand members.[32] By the end of that year the novel had sold two hundred thousand copies and, as one historian writes, it caused millions of Americans—"social workers, farmers, businessmen, bankers, and housewives"—to confront Bellamy's "argument for a wholesale rearrangement of their capitalist society."[33] Gaston, according to a friend, was "much pleased with the book," but his club was not formally affiliated with the Bellamy movement.[34] Nevertheless, the great author's advice was solicited and he was invited to come to Des Moines to speak to its members. Pleading poor health, Bellamy declined the invitation, praised Gaston as one who was "looking for the morning," and counselled him to "do all you can for our common cause personally and in your paper," assuring him that "you can in no other way serve your country better."[35]

The most popular novel of social criticism since *Uncle Tom's Cabin*, Bellamy's *Looking Backward* viewed the America of the 1880s from the perspective of the year 2000, the time its hero awakened after more than

Opposite: Edward Bellamy's letter encouraging E.B. Gaston.

24

Chicopee Falls Mass
April 17
1880

Ernest B. Gaston

Dear Sir

Your letter
of March 11 would have been answered
more promptly but for sickness
and absence. I am sorry
to disappoint any who are, with me,
looking for the morning, but
I am obliged at present to
decline all lecturing engage-
ments. Do all you can
for our common cause per-
sonally and in your paper.
I am sure you can in no other way
serve your country better

truly yrs

Edward Bellamy

a century's sleep. Gaston and his fellow Investigating Club members could sympathize with Bellamy's Julian West, a man of culture and comfortable means who was appalled by the realities of his own age, viewed with fresh eyes. They could also agree with the sage Dr. Leete, West's twenty-first century host and mentor, who analyzed for him the doomed social order of the nineteenth century. The central problem, Dr. Leete explained, was "excessive individualism." A cancer destroying the country, it was the "animating idea" of the age; it was a foil to "public spirit" and was "fatal to any vital sentiment of brotherhood and common interest among living men" as well as subversive of "any realization of the responsibility of the living for the generation to follow." With unbridled individualism fueling and guiding the fabulous industrial and technological revolution, American workers lost the independence and control over their destiny they had once had, and, in the face of "the absorption of business by ever larger monopolies," the small businesses that were not sucked into the vortex of monopoly "were reduced to the condition of rats and mice, living in holes and corners, and counting on evading notice for the enjoyment of existence." When Dr. Leete explained that "the records of the period show that the outcry against the concentration of capital was furious," the incipient Des Moines rebels could take heart, feeling that their voices contributed to that outcry; they were part of a movement.[36]

According to Bellamy's utopian romance, the great outcry had produced change without revolution. There was no class warfare. Instead, enlightened citizens came to regard socialism as beneficent, humane, and rational, and saw it as a logical alternative to the ruthless, competitive industrial order of capitalism. A peaceful, evolutionary process took the consolidation that had been the distinguishing feature

26

of the nineteenth century industrial revolution to its logical conclusion so that all competing industries had been absorbed by a "single syndicate representing the people, to be conducted in the common interest for the common profit." With the means of production and distribution nationalized, inefficiency was eliminated along with exploitation and inequality. National income rose and individual incomes, once wildly uneven, became more nearly equal. Such a vision had great appeal. The reform-minded Iowa *Tribune* explained approvingly that the Bellamy doctrine meant "ownership and control of capital, and the organization and direction of labor by the Nation." Nationalism, the term Bellamy preferred to socialism, would guarantee "to every citizen nurture, education and comfortable maintenance from the cradle to the grave."[37]

Gaston and his friends studied Henry George as well as Bellamy. George had entered into the American consciousness a decade earlier with the publication of *Progress and Poverty*, an eloquent work that combined economics and ethics, laid bare the inequities of the social order, and made its reformation appear not only urgently needed but also possible. Described by George's biographer as "a moral Mount Whitney of American protest," *Progress and Poverty* was unmatched in its power to gather converts to radicalism and protest.[38] "No single figure in the last two decades of the nineteenth century was more successful than Henry George in arousing public opinion to an awareness of the social origins of wealth and poverty," one historian writes, while another believes that his writings "magically catalyzed the best yearnings" of the men and women of the 'eighties, helping to banish the arrogance and indifference of the previous generation.[39] The famous writer, also a powerful orator, spoke in the Opera House in Des Moines in January of 1889 but no record survives to tell whether Gaston heard or met him.[40]

To George the central problems of the age were the unfair distribution of wealth and power and the deepening poverty that accompanied unprecedented material progress. "This association of poverty with progress," he wrote in his most famous passage, "is the great enigma of our times. . . . It is the riddle which the Sphinx of Fate puts to our civilization and which not to answer is to be destroyed." Why, George asked, and his Des Moines readers wondered, could not everyone benefit from society's prodigious wealth-producing ability? Advancing material progress ought "to improve the condition of the lowest class in the essentials of healthy, happy life," he wrote; instead, it made life worse for millions of people. Not to discover and then to apply a solution to this problem, George warned, was to ensure the decline of American civilization:

> What has destroyed every previous civilization has been the tendency to the unequal distribution of wealth and power. This same tendency, operating with increasing force, is observable in our civilization today, showing itself in every progressive community, and with greater intensity the more progressive the community. Wages and interest tend constantly to fall, rent to rise, the rich to become very much richer, the poor to become more helpless and hopeless, and the middle class to be swept away.[41]

As members of the threatened middle class, their consciences stirred by the poor who "become more helpless and hopeless," Gaston and his friends pored over the works of George and Bellamy in the winter of 1889-1890. The two prophets, despite sharply different styles, wrote generally similar descriptions of the problem that cried out for solution. Each also wrote with a moral urgency that made ardent reformers of readers throughout the nation and abroad as well. The differing programs of action they offered to those converted readers, however, clashed in what appeared to be fundamental ways.[42] Bellamy saw a logical development in the history of capital consolidation and favored national ownership and control of the means of production and distribution, a form of socialism he and his followers called nationalism. George, anguished by the same excessive individualism that outraged Bellamy, believed that its evils could be curbed, the spirit of cooperation nurtured, and the productivity of free individuals enlarged by socializing land, the one factor of production whose monopoly he believed accounted for poverty amidst plenty. "We have examined all the remedies, short of the abolition of private property in land," he wrote, "and have found them all inefficacious or impracticable. . . . Poverty deepens as wealth increases, and wages are forced down while productive power grows," he explained, "because land, which is the source of all wealth and the field of all labor, is monopolized." Thus, to abolish poverty and make wages just, he concluded, "*We must make land common property.*"[43]

Two years before Gaston and his friends began studying George, the radical message of *Progress and Poverty* had been somewhat muted by some of George's least-radical followers who came up with the deceptive label "single tax." Fearing popular objection to land nationalization, wishing to enlist businessmen in their cause, and unable to find an appropriate title for their movement, these Georgists argued that it was necessary only to nationalize the income from land, through taxation;

Henry George

land titles could remain undisturbed. All government revenue could be raised by such a tax on community-created land values, they believed, removing the justification for any other form of taxation—thus the label "single tax." George himself "never regarded the term as describing his philosophy," his son wrote, "but rather as indicating the method he would take to apply it."[44]

Put differently, George saw the single tax as the fundamental reform, the basic structural change, that would make possible the flowering of his philosophy. The philosophy itself went far beyond a change in tax policy. George's understanding of the subtle relationship between competition and cooperation and his awareness of society's increasing complexity kept him from simple doctrinal solutions. He opposed a heavy government hand on individual initiative, but he advocated new cooperative functions. Putting it bluntly in his 1883 book, *Social Problems*, George wrote that "either government must manage the railroads or the railroads must manage the government." And he added: "all I have said of the railroad applies . . . to the telegraph, the telephone, the supplying of cities with gas, water, heat and electricity,—in short to all businesses which are in their nature monopolies."[45]

Gaston was profoundly influenced by George's writings, and in time George would become the chief intellectual force in his life. But, at this early stage of his development, Gaston did not view *Progress and Poverty* as an exclusive guide to reform. Though persuaded of the iniquity of land monopoly, he still was convinced that socialized production and distribution were required in the ideal community.

Gaston's socialist inclinations, nurtured by his reading of *Looking Backward*, may have been fortified by another book the group read that winter, Laurence Gronlund's *The Cooperative Commonwealth*. Published in 1884, it never rivaled *Looking Backward* or *Progress and Poverty* in either influence or sales, but its Danish-born author believed he was the first writer to explain to an American audience the essentials of Marxian socialism. According to Gronlund, the Marxian road to socialism did not require class conflict. Instead, Gronlund described a scheme of evolutionary, peaceful development that led to a cooperative commonwealth in which the state would help "every individual to attain the highest development he or she has capacity for," a state that would "lay a cover for every one at Nature's table." To lead the peaceful revolution, Gronlund called for the mobilization of "a vigorous . . . minority of intelligent and energetic American men and women," mostly young people like Gaston and his associates in the Investigating Club. Bellamy believed that Gronlund would lodge too much power in the hands of the working class, complaining that "the germ of this coming order Mr. Gronlund professes to see in the trades union, while the nationalists see it in the nation."[46]

The eclectic reading habits of the Investigating Club members were typical of reformers of Gaston's generation. Theirs was an age when heightened conscience, shocked and galvanized by the brutal realities of social change, was fortunately coupled with unusual flexibility—in ideas, in movements, and in social experiments. Ideas were in flux and ideological lines were constantly being tested and redrawn. Karl Marx, for example, was but one of many socialist writers; and, in fact, he had very little influence in America. Bellamy had never studied either Marx or German socialism when he wrote *Looking Backward* and, as the historian John Thomas puts it, he "snorted derisively" when his failure to discuss Marx was mentioned. The very word socialism, in fact, was a relative newcomer to the English language and still had uncertain meaning. Thus, intellectual excitement and hopes for change flourished because they were free of the blinding mental associations and reminders of failed doctrines that would later constrict social analysis.[47]

Dorothy Ross has written of the "transforming enthusiasm of the early eighties" when "evangelical, liberal, and socialist impulses converged on the desire for a more egalitarian and fraternal order." Most of the young intellectuals who spoke of "socialism," as Ross explains, understood it to mean "the principle of association or cooperation in economic and political life." It was the opposite of individualism, which meant the pursuit of self interest, unrestrained by considerations for society as a whole. Definitions of socialism were varied enough to include "the voluntary efforts of workingmen to combine into cooperative industries as well as efforts of the state to control economic activity on behalf of all classes." With such an elastic meaning, the banner of socialism was lifted by reformers all across the country.[48]

This helps us to understand why, as Daniel T. Rodgers explains, there could be a pronounced harmony of interest among reformers hawking all manner of apparently competing solutions. They were united in a common quest by "a vivid sense of exploitation," as he puts it. One of Bellamy's biographers describes the era as "a period of feeling about for a good social order," a time when rival social reformers were more drawn together by their common outrage rather than separated by their differing social philosophies. Henry George's biographer writes of the many threads of reform that were being woven into a common design. "The Henry George impulse," Charles Barker explains, "interfiliated with other impulses. . . . Such a cross-connecting . . . was never more natural than during . . . the last quarter of the nineteenth century." With deep faith in his own political economy, George himself deplored the union of disparate ideas. But with no such fixed intellectual anchor, Gaston and his associates read and learned from Bellamy, George, Gronlund, and others, drawing inspiration and insight from all of them, all the while choosing freely what suited them best. [49]

At some point the club members shifted the focus from ideas to action. What could be done? They had reached agreement about what was wrong, and they were getting closer to a vision of what a reconstructed nation might look like. They were clear about the need for a more caring, cooperative society, one that would nurture individual expression and achievement as it looked to the common welfare. But what might a few individual reformers do to stem the onslaught of greed and chart a new course for their country? Could they be more than thoughtful observers and vigilant critics of their society? Were they foolish to think it really possible for a few ordinary citizens to make a difference in the historical process? How could one make a difference? What options did America offer?

The labor movement and the political process were the two most obvious ones. Gaston was strongly drawn to the Knights of Labor, now twenty years old and beginning to recede from the crest of its influence. Like Henry George, who had joined the Knights in 1883, Gaston lauded the view of land as "the natural source of wealth" and "the heritage of all the people." As the nation's most influential organization of working men and women, the Knights championed the same "religion of solidarity" emphasized by Bellamy and the same belief in the evolution of natural cooperation favored by George. Opposing inequality and exploitation in American life, especially disparate wage scales for women, child labor abuses, and discrimination against blacks, the Knights pointed the way to a cooperative commonwealth by favoring the eight-hour day, a graduated income tax, and public ownership of such "natural monopolies" as railroads, telephones, and telegraphs. The famous Knights' declaration that "an injury to one is the concern of all" expressed a value system that stood in stark contrast to the acquisitive, competitive individualism of the emerging corporate state.[50]

Gaston sympathized with the Knights' concept of a cooperative society but he sensed it was not enough, at least not for him, and so he looked elsewhere for what he hoped would be a more comprehensive way of advancing the ideas he and his friends had been studying. He had been active in local politics since his university days, but at the end of the 1880s he seems not to have considered politics a hopeful avenue to reform. He had not joined either the Greenback Party or the Union Labor Party, the two radical alternatives available to him. Instead, he remained a member of the Republican Party, but he grew increasingly disillusioned both with its retreat from its former idealism and with the American political system in general.[51]

IV

The Communitarian Alternative

REJECTING BOTH POLITICS AND THE LABOR MOVE-
ment as the forums for their reformist impulses, Gaston and
his friends found the direction they were seeking in the country's
rich communitarian tradition. Here they found what they believed
would be a practical means of putting their ideas into practice.

For at least a century dissatisfied and idealistic Americans, men
and women with utopian dreams and bold plans, had tried out their
ideas in experimental communities. They had created self-contained
societies set apart from the larger world, established as a haven for
themselves and as models of what the larger society might become.
Some of these communities, like New Harmony and Brook Farm, had
become internationally famous demonstrations of the ideas of Robert
Owen and of Charles Fourier, the two most prominent theoreticians of
communitarian socialism. These and other pre-Civil War experiments
were inspirations to many of Gaston's contemporaries. They believed
that such experiments were especially relevant in the 1880s. The idea of
"reform by nucleation," as one historian puts it, "held promise for a
new generation of reformers."[52] Albert Brisbane, a follower of Fourier
and one of the most famous of the antebellum communitarians, had

expressed the hope of communitarinism this way: "The reform we contemplate . . . will change quietly and by substitution what is false and defective. . . . It can moreover be tried on a small scale, and it will only spread when practice has shown its superiority over the present system."[53]

Gaston probably made no count of the number of communitarian experiments that had been tried, and scholars today differ in their estimates, but a cautious historian might hazard that over two hundred had been established in the previous hundred years. Reading the reform press and exchanging letters with community builders in other parts of the country, Gaston was excited by accounts of new efforts. His own age, he believed, was wonderfully suited for a new flowering of the communitarian tradition.[54]

Two colonies emerging from the ferment of that decade particularly appealed to Gaston, and the Investigating Club studied them carefully. The first was the Credit Foncier of Sinaloa, founded in 1886 by Albert Kimsey Owen at Topolobampo Bay on the west coast of Mexico. Based on a plan called "integral cooperation," Owen's colony combined influences of Fourier and his French disciple, Jean-Baptiste André Godin, with his own swashbuckling socialism. Owen dreamed of servicing freight and passenger traffic from the United States to China by creating a great Pacific City as the terminus of a transcontinental railroad. He won financial backing from the Kansas socialist millionaire Christian B. Hoffman and journalistic support from the feminist novelist and communitarian reformer Marie Howland and her husband, Edward Howland. The appeal of Topolobampo to Gaston—at least the description of what it was to be that he read in Owen's book *Integral Cooperation*—is easy to understand. In these pages he learned of the plans for achieving harmony and equality through socialized production and distribution, cooperative housekeeping and child rearing, broad avenues and spacious public parks—a perfect integration of architecture and ideology that would blossom in a rich intellectual and cultural life. Gaston never went to Topolobampo, but he learned later of a reality that was painfully different from the dream. Primitive physical facilities strained daily life and the cooperative spirit was regularly vitiated by petty human jealousies, conflicting personal values, and power struggles that presaged the colony's demise in the 1890s. He would learn from both the dream and the reality.[55]

A second, and more important, model that Gaston chose to study was the Kaweah Cooperative Colony Company of Tulare County, California. Established in a forest of giant sequoias in 1886, Kaweah advertised itself to be "a practical democratic co-operative commonwealth founded upon the principles of Laurence Gronlund's 'Cooperative Commonwealth' and Edward Bellamy's 'Looking Backward.'" The driving forces behind it were Burnette G. Haskell and James J. Martin, San Francisco labor leaders. Haskell, the more influential of the two, claimed to be a Marxist and an anarchist. Both men were inspired by Gronlund's *Cooperative Commonwealth*, and late in 1884 they and sixty-eight of their followers drew up plans for a colony based on a scheme of hierarchical democracy advocated by Gronlund—election of officers from below, by the workers, and removal from above by superiors. The constitution also provided for an elaborate array of industrial departments to assure accountability for every colony activity, and an equalitarian system of rewards. All labor received thirty cents an hour; those who did not work were not paid. Payment was not in cash, but in time-checks, a unit of credit stated in minutes worked, that formed a circulating medium within the colony. Modified and simplified with experience, the organizational scheme that Gaston studied in 1890 appeared to him to be democratic enough, with ultimate power residing in the membership, and he spoke approvingly of the general plan for cooperative production and distribution.[56]

Bellamy became a second intellectual guide for the Kaweahans after *Looking Backward* was published. While Gronlund became a non-resident member, Bellamy, according to the colony's historian, "shook his head over Kaweah; no such experiment," he thought, "could succeed on less than a national scale." Bellamy's followers, many of whom translated his teachings into communitarian efforts, were obviously not of a mind with their mentor and a goodly number of them made their way to California to join the colony, share in the hardships of pioneer life and relax under the huge sequoia they called the Karl Marx Tree.

Gaston eagerly read accounts of the experiment and unsuccessfully attempted to swap advertising in his newspaper for rail transportation to San Francisco. Although he was unable to raise money to visit Kaweah, he continued to be enthusiastic about the colony's "admirable plan" and proclaimed it to be of interest to "all who are studying the social and industrial problem of the day." By the end of 1890, however, word reached him of bitter quarrels in the colony as well as material setbacks. "I have followed with sorrow the development of the dissensions in Kaweah," Gaston wrote. "I believe its founders to be men of pure and lofty aims, . . . but the mind capable of planning is not always capable of executing."[57]

Young though he was, Gaston thought of himself as the kind of practical idealist who could both plan and execute. That faith would

DIVISION OF COMMONWEAL,
DEP'T OF ADMINISTRATION,
BUREAU OF THE EXECUTIVE,

The Secretary's Office.

J. J. Martin, Secretary.

Visalia, Cal. July 8, 1890

In Reply to yours of
..................., 189...

Ernest B. Gaston Esq
Des Moines

Dear Sir

Replying to your favor of 1st inst I regret your _____ should have been omitted from the Exchange list, and have now rectified this — Should have been pleased to have your visit, but heartily wish you success in forming a new Colony — Unless you have a special reason for selecting Louisiana I should not Consider it a desirable location. A more Exhilarating climate would seem to me desirable, if not absolutely essential to the success of such an undertaking.

very truly Yours

J. J. Martin Secty

Letter from the Kaweah Co-Operative Colony.

39

now meet its first test. By July 1890, he and his friends had put on paper and were ready to publicize the blueprint for their own utopia. The Des Moines newspapers carried long descriptions of their proposed "National Co-operative Company" and before the month was out press notices had appeared in perhaps a score of other cities, most of them announcing a new attempt to institute the "Bellamy Plan."[58] News of the projected colony excited interest throughout the country; soon cards and letters were pouring into Des Moines, asking for particulars, sharing with Gaston tales of exploitation and distress, and expressing a deep faith in cooperation. Gaston was obviously moved by the wave of interest and the extent of human suffering and injustice it bespoke. He would not forget these letters.

From Germany came a plea to be permitted to join in the effort to implement "Bellamy's excellent ideas," promising warm enthusiasm from "thousands of efficient industrious Europeans, slaves of the capitalists who are thirsting for freedom." A Russian immigrant wrote from Kansas City that he had already lost his child, wife, and property, that he was going more deeply into debt, was "cracked" in health, and had "come to bedrock." He said he would "thank my God if you, friends of humanity, will give me chance to associate with you in this great movement for delivering humanity from beasthood to humanity." Another European immigrant, whose home and mill had been burned down by the Jesse and Frank James gang, wrote from New Orleans of his struggle to maintain his socialist principles. He hoped he would receive his "reward by getting a chance to work with you."[59] Letters from these immigrants, who had come to America to find greater freedom and opportunity, underscored the ironic fate America held for them.

By October, upwards of a hundred persons from twenty-one states had written to express interest.[60] Most were native born—workingmen, tradesmen, and farmers. All but two or three were men. Some wrote eloquently; some had difficulty spelling or forming their letters correctly; a few were veterans of other cooperative colony ventures; and some wrote learnedly about the advantages of competing economic doctrines. All agreed that the United States was not the land of opportunity its resources, mythology, and history intended it to be. To see America through their eyes touched the young idealist who received their letters; it also deepened his resolve to find the explanation for their grief and the answer to their plight.

Gaston wrote long and solicitous letters to most of these correspondents. Taking on the job of colony secretary, he meticulously made copies of his replies in a newly acquired journal.[61] These were heady months for Gaston as he engaged for the first time the minds and hearts of those who, he hoped, would be the sinew of his practical demonstration of a new route to the cooperative commonwealth.

He and Clara had two children by this time, after the birth of James Ernest in June. But the increased family responsibilities do not seem to have either altered his course or slowed him down, if one is to judge from the many long and thoughtful letters he drafted, often late in the night after his family had gone to sleep. These letters reveal a man possessed by his mission. In them he mixed soaring enthusiasm for the colony venture—"the almost universal opinion of those who have studied our plan is that it is the simplest, best, and most practical ever put forth"—with fearful warnings of the evil it must combat. Every day, in fact, the threat to the nation was growing stronger and more menacing he believed. In replying to one letter, he wrote of "individualism and competition gone to *seed"* as the defining characteristic of the country; people were rewarded for selfish activities in a society that not only approved but depended upon the subjugation of the many to the few. The "present competitive system," he wrote to another prospective member, allowed individuals to engage in whatever they believed they "can get money out of without regard to the needs of the community." Success came by levying tribute on their fellow citizens "through control of natural opportunities," by becoming monopolists. "One of the worst fruits of the present system," he said to another prospective colonist, was the way it drained the sense of self-worth out of many honest people, robbing them "of all confidence in . . . humanity." He admonished his brother-in-law, a mildly skeptical merchant, telling him that it was not possible, under the existing competitive system, for "a man to do business a day without being compelled to do things which are repugnant to his moral sense."[62]

The antidote to such a corrupt and degrading economic order, Gaston wrote, was a system in which society—the human community as a whole—would "conduct all business and hold all natural opportunities in trust for the benefit of all." By "natural opportunities" he meant natural resources, especially land, a reflection of his debt to George. The aim of the National Cooperative Company would be to show, on a small scale, how such a society would function.

Surviving descriptions of the National Cooperative Company are vague and derivitative, drawing heavily on the constitution of the Kaweah Company. The plan was to purchase a large tract of land, probably in southwest Louisiana, that would be the common property of all the members. The Company would somehow achieve economic self sufficency through agricultural and manufacturing enterprises it would later select. Collective decisions would determine what specific tasks would be performed by which workers; a uniform wage scale would be adopted; and the Company would devise a system of credit and distribution which would free it of reliance on the outside world. The construction of homes and public buildings was also to be a communal undertaking, with community values reflected in the structures in which people lived and worked. In all of these activities, women and men would stand on an equal footing, thus aligning Gaston's colony with the struggle for women's rights, at a time when women were everywhere disfranchised. Finally, schools and intellectual and artistic endeavors would be collectively planned and implemented to bind the colonists together, reinforcing their sense of common purpose. They would then "propagate and extend in the world at large the idea of universal and just co-operation."[63]

The colony was frequently described as an attempt to make a practical application of Bellamy's utopian ideas. Many of those inquiring about details assumed that to be the case and, in fact, were drawn precisely because of their attachment to Bellamy's ideas. Gaston objected to so close an identification, however, because it obscured a vital difference between his emerging social philosophy and that of Bellamy as well as other cooperative-colony schemes. The difference came from contrasting ideas regarding motivation and fairness and was expressed in rival ways of determining wages. Bellamy's famous socialist doctrine—"from each according to his ability, to each according to his need"—had a ring of justice to it, Gaston conceded, but in the real world, even a world restructured by good reformers, it would be impossible to determine whether individuals actually worked according to their abilities or to measure the extent of their needs. "The finite mind," he wrote, "can only judge from visible *results*." Thus, he would cast aside Bellamy's formula and substitute for it a structure that would cater more to individual differences and initiatives: "All will have equal opportunity and each will be rewarded according to his deeds."[64]

This argument of Gaston's was characteristic of what Daniel Rodgers describes as the dominant radical viewpoint of the age, the belief that "a man's reward ought to match the labor he expended." Translated into Company practice, this would mean that enterprises cooperatively conceived and managed would reward laborers differently, according to what they produced, which in turn would be a reflection of their skill and their application, but never of special privilege. To do otherwise, he believed (and he cited the examples of several cooperative ventures where he saw this happen), would be to reduce "the diligent and ambitious to the same level of living and reward as the indolent and unambitious," thus creating, ironically, another form of special privilege. In addition, he believed that what he called the "extreme socialist" system would "destroy individuality and crush the strongest desire of the human heart to lift itself above its fellows."[65]

Rejecting what he called Bellamy's "extreme socialism," and acknowledging what he believed was a universal competitive urge, he likewise found problems with Henry George's more individualistic philosophy. Obviously impressed by George, Gaston wrote that land monopoly put labor "at the mercy of our individualistic capitalistic system of production" with the result that labor "must take the pittance offered by capital, which hovers all the time close around the point of subsistence." And he believed it "a truth so evident as to need no demonstration that *use* gives the only right to control of land." Legal titles to land, he said, were "no more evidence of *moral right* than the bills of sale by which the unfortunate blacks were held in bondage but a few years since in our own land." It was a powerful analogy—the suggestion that human slavery and land monopoly were moral equivalents. It also revealed again the influence of George, who had linked the two in *Progress and Poverty* as twin injustices and he added that "the ownership of land will always give the ownership of men." None of this, however, led Gaston to believe the single tax was an adequate exclusive reform. He was, he said in a letter discussing George's theories, "a firm believer in Socialism in production and distribution."[66] Gaston's prospective colony thus fell between Bellamy's "extreme socialism" and George's modified individualism.

With the theoretical framework outlined, all of Gaston's energies now turned to the practical details of recruiting members, choosing a site, and laying plans for settlement. At times he seemed awed by the prospects of leading a group of settlers to their promised land, writing to one man: "I will be but 29 years old this month and have thought seriously about this question but a short time."[67] But he never let his youth and inexperience stop him. He visited prospective sites in Louisiana at the end of the summer and established contacts with real estate agents there. Louisiana was chosen because founding members had special contacts there which they believed should be pursued.[68] No inquiries seem to have gone to other areas. Gaston's correspondence with agents after he returned to Iowa reveals indecision and insufficient funds with which to acquire anything like the needed acreage. Soon his frustration began to mount over the failure to apply for membership of those who had written letters of interest. By October 15, the first date set for the trip South, only two persons had been added to the four original

Des Moines organizers by paying the five dollar down payment on their $500 membership.[69]

Though discouraged, Gaston had a ready explanation. "There is no lack of good men thoroughly convinced of the practicability of our plan and anxious to join us," he wrote, "but they have not as yet been able to get ready." Most were poor. Those who had property could not sell it because of a depression in the real estate market. Letter after letter refers to hard times and the inability of prospective members to sell property to raise cash. Still others held back, saying they would come once the colony had proved itself. To make matters worse, Gaston began to suspect in September that E. D. Smith, one of the charter members, was unreliable. By November he had "abundant reason" for doubting Smith's commitment and he soon concluded that the man "was never interested in the Colony idea except for the opportunities he thought he saw for outside speculation." As winter came to Des Moines, disappointment piled on top of disappointment. By December he had to admit that the lack of applications for membership doomed his dream, at least in its present form and for the present moment. On December 1 he wrote that "we have given up for the present our cherished plan." Characteristically, however, he added: "I have never been more determined to put our plans into execution and I will never give up until I see them tried."[70]

It was not easy to admit defeat. On the day after Christmas, he wrote to one friend that "prevailing hard times" had kept them from getting the colony established, but he hoped "to do so ere long." Several months later, at the end of May, he wrote to A. K. Owen of the Topolobampo colony telling Owen of his effort, explaining that it failed because "the kind of people who are attracted to such an enterprise are

. . . poor and suffering from existing conditions." But he was "still determined . . . to 'seek refuge' in a Cooperative Society." By then, though, he thought he might join someone else's rather than try again to form his own.[71]

Meanwhile, there was the matter of earning a living and finding creative outlets for his zeal to make a difference in the world. Income from the *Advocate* was not enough to live on, and he had rejected his real estate business. He apparently sold some of the land he had purchased earlier for development, and that tided him over. It obviously was not enough, however, for he spent a good part of the winter months in Nebraska and Kansas selling medical publications from D. Appleton publishers. Before spring came Clara was pregnant; a third child was on the way.[72]

V

The Populist Experience

WHEN GASTON WROTE IN MAY 1891 TO TELL OWEN of his continuing interest in communitarian reform he had already opened a new chapter of his career as a reformer. The first indication of his new commitment appeared in the March 4 issue of the *Tribune*. The recently formed National Citizens' Industrial Alliance, said to have "so ably seconded the farmers of Kansas in their fight against the hosts of organized monopoly," was coming to Iowa. The first local assembly had already been formed and a mass meeting at the Opera House was planned for March 13. The *Tribune* believed it would be "the most important political meeting in the capital city for years." Those wanting more information were advised to write to the secretary of the new local, E. B. Gaston.[73]

A large and eager audience came to the Opera House on the 13th to hear speeches and take inspiration. Among the prominent men on the platform, none was more admired than General James B. Weaver. Along with E. H. Gillette he was co-owner of the *Tribune*. Both Weaver and Gillette were veteran reformers and former Congressmen. Weaver, the 1880 presidential candidate on the Greenback Party ticket, was now leading the surging agrarian revolt that had engendered the Citizens'

Alliance.

The first speech of the evening was given by Weaver's friend Professor James Bellangee, a single-tax advocate who would become a shaping figure in Gaston's future career. Known to his admirers as the Junius of Des Moines, Bellangee spoke of the spreading "discontent and wretchedness" in the nation, declaring that "the ruling class look upon one as a crime and the other as a misfortune." Former Senator Charles H. Van Wyck of Nebraska, the featured speaker of the evening, attacked the myths he believed were manipulated to quiet the dispossessed and stroke the egos of the oppressors. "We have been taught to believe we have a superior civilization," he said, with "greater education, equal privileges to all, free and universal suffrage," and "that every citizen, however humble, is sovereign; that our government is of, by and for the people." None of this, he roared, was true. A revolution was in the making, and the next step was to form a new political party to accomplish it. Everyone present, and many others who could not attend, agreed. Some of the absent friends wrote congratulatory letters which secretary Gaston read aloud in his resonating bass voice.[74]

The cause Gaston now took up was about to become one of the great mass movements for social change in American history, with a recruiting power far beyond the reach of the small and isolated colonies of communitarian reformers to whom he had so recently committed himself.[75] The movement had been in the making for more than a generation. The rapid industrial and technological changes in America in the decades after the Civil War altered the way people made livings, how and where they lived, and transformed the cultural assumptions that had defined their images of themselves and their country. The nation's farmers, especially those who grew staple crops in the South and West, felt rejected, victimized rather than rewarded, by the great release of new wealth-producing activities and labor-saving devices.[76] Their plight was complicated by an unfavorable international market in which their crops commanded less while their costs rose. In these straitened circumstances a literature of protest and hope arose to channel the anger and despair felt by so many farmers.

Hamlin Garland, one of Gaston's new comrades, gave eloquent voice to their deeper concerns. His first book of short stories, *Main-Travelled Roads*, appeared in the spring of 1891. Capturing in homely detail a way of life that was too often lonely and disappointing, he made vivid the courage and dignity of embattled men and women, struggling "under the lion's paw." One of his characters, sounding almost like an alliance speaker, told of "fifty per cent of these farms mortgaged, in spite of the labors of every member of the family and the most frugal living."[77]

Farmers had banded together since the 1860s, searching for effective ways to organize and to express their viewpoints. They founded an organization called the Patrons of Husbandry, which was known familiarly as the Grange, to unite farmers for both economic action and social activities. In the 1880s they created organizations called alliances to further their interests—the Northern Alliance, the Southern Alliance, and the Colored Alliance.[78] Earlier farmer protests had led to the formation of the Greenback Party in the 1870s, but the alliances of the 1880s hoped to achieve their reforms through challenges within the existing two-party system. The Southern Alliance, which had won the allegiance of Weaver and the *Tribune*, stunned southern Democrats with successes in the 1890 state elections, but a year later the prospects for genuine change of the sort the farmers wanted seemed distant.

A series of tempestuous conferences brought together alliance members along with representatives of virtually every known reform group and ideology in the country, to share ideas, issue increasingly radical demands, and again debate the wisdom of forming a third party. One delegate to the "National Union Conference" in Cincinnati in May 1891, confessed that it was the fifth meeting he had attended to discuss the formation of a new party.[79] He and others who shared his view were to be disappointed no longer. The People's Party of the United States was all but formed at that Cincinnati gathering and, as the meeting in the Des Moines Opera House in March had indicated, sentiment was strong for the formation of a state party. After the Cincinnati meeting, forming a new state party became the main political business in Iowa. Gaston was one of those who issued the call for a "People's Independent State Convention" to meet in Des Moines on June 3.[80]

The notices of these political meetings in the *Tribune* may well have been written by Gaston himself. Sometime in the spring of 1891 he joined the editorial staff at what was undoubtedly a modest salary. No references to the *Suburban Advocate* survive to let us know when he abandoned it, but a good guess would be that he either sold it or let it fold when he was well established in his new job. For the next two and a half years his life was bound up with his new colleagues at the paper and with the new political party he and they championed. The *Tribune* became the informal general headquarters of the Iowa Populist Party as well as its major voice. The offices teemed with people and ideas, giving Gaston a unique opportunity to broaden his network of reform-minded friends. He also improved his journalistic skills, developed his leadership abilities, and refined his social analysis.[81]

General Weaver, who was fifty-eight when Gaston joined the *Tribune*, inspired him. According to one historian, Weaver was "utterly incorruptible," with a "commanding presence and fiery oratory."[82] He also was a powerful writer in whose prose Gaston found ringing confirmation of his own indictments of the emerging corporate state. "The spirit of the corporation," Weaver wrote, "is aggressive and essentially warlike." It had seized the "sovereign functions" of government—"a shameful betrayal of a sacred trust"—and had used them "for the accumulation of vast and overshadowing private fortunes." The "melancholy contrasts of wealth and poverty, of individual happiness and widespread infelicity" were part of a huge contradiction of the great promise with which the Republic was born. The "leading spirits" of his own age, Weaver declared, "are entrenched behind class laws and revel in special privilege." To overthrow them would require a second American revolution. "That revolution," he be-

General James B. Weaver, editor of the *Farmer's Tribune* and 1892 Populist presidential candidate.

lieved, "is upon us even now."[83] With Weaver as his friend and mentor, Gaston felt he was part of that revolution. When Weaver died two decades later, Gaston wrote that "the people never had a truer friend than he . . . . He was a man of great ability as orator and debater able to hold his own. . . in any company and had a genial and sympathetic personality which compelled the deepest and most enduring friendships."[84]

The city's leading daily characterized the Populist protest as the work of "a medley of malcontents, one-idea hobbyists, unreasonable fiatists, . . . 'born-tired' extremists, and blatant demagogues."[85] But General Weaver's young men at the *Tribune*, perhaps even flattered by these calumnies, saw themselves and their cause differently. Filled with enthusiasm and idealism, they hailed the National Union Conference at Cincinnati as "one of the most remarkable ever assembled in America," opening a "new epoch in the history of the United States." One of Gaston's friends wrote from Texas that "the contest will be fierce . . . but the victory will be glorious." And one of the paper's editors proclaimed that "the supreme moment in this experiment of popular government is rapidly approaching."[86]

The National Citizens' Industrial Alliance Gaston promoted was designed to provide a forum for those who were not eligible for membership in the Farmers' Alliance—including journalists like himself—to forge a bond between town and country, farmer and businessman, tenant and factory worker.[87] Given his interest in poverty and his recent study of Bellamy and George, it is hardly surprising that Gaston welcomed the chance to see in the farmers' revolt a broad national reform movement. He was probably cheered when he read in the *Tribune* that Bellamy's *New Nation* was "outspoken in its advocacy of the People's party" and he may have read Bellamy's own comment in the magazine that "the *New Nation* welcomes the peoples' party into the field of national politics." George, on the other hand, withheld his support. Although he conceded that "widespread and well founded discontent" had given rise to the party, he dismissed its platform as mere "patchwork."[88]

George's dismissal of Populism stemmed partly from judgments that were "sectarian and ungenerous," according to his chief biographer. Another scholar says he assumed "the role of spoiler of the People's party hopes" because he believed that Populists, like Bellamy, had too strong an "impulse to socialism." But George also criticized Populists because he believed their reform program lacked a coherent philosophy and because they believed land should be private property. For their part, many Populists rejected George. They resented being told that private property in land was immoral and they wrongly suspected that the single tax would increase the tax burden on farmers.[89]

Gaston, partly at Bellangee's urging, was at this time coming increasingly to admire George's theories but, not yet thirty years old, he was still testing many different ideas. He embraced Populism partly because he believed in most of its principles, but also because he correctly understood that no other movement offered reformers such opportunities for success. It was, he sensed, a moment and a movement not to be missed.

Hamlin Garland agreed. A year older than Gaston, Garland had spent part of his boyhood in Iowa. He returned in 1891, just as he was beginning to gain literary fame, on a mission to write about the agrarian uprising. Skeptical of the Farmers' Alliance when he began his inquiry—he said that he "regarded its methods as doubtful, and its aims as foolish, if not worse"—he soon began working for the state central committee of the Iowa party, campaigning for its candidates in the fall elections. Garland's conversion was important because he came to Populism as a passionate Georgist. He championed the single tax in lectures and articles and shaped many of his plays, poems, and stories to illustrate it. The Georgist press praised "Under the Lion's Paw," his most famous story, for the way it exposed "in very vivid colors the whole question of landlordism." With such single-minded concentration on the single-tax doctrine, Garland surprised even himself when he met the young men leading the Iowa insurgency. "They are alive to new ideas," he reported. "They eagerly heard me in advocacy of the single tax." He came to find in these young and crusading idealists something that must have reminded him of himself. He found a "glowing hope" in them and their war "against the three great fundamental monopolies—the monopoly of land, the monopoly of transportation, and the monopoly of money." Soon he was lecturing to the Chicago Single Tax Club about the need for single taxers everywhere to support the Populist revolt. That particular mission was mostly a failure, but Garland's example no doubt fortified Gaston's commitment.[90]

Gaston longed for an inclusive reform movement, one that would draw on the theories of both George and Bellamy, and one that would speak to the aspirations of factory workers and farmers, country folk and city-dwellers. The fundamental truth about the Populist revolt, however, was that its demands were all shaped by specific rural experiences. Commonly expressed as a revolt against the triple monopoly of which Garland spoke—the monopoly of land, money, and transportation—the Populist reforms aimed to democratize the economic institutions that intruded most directly in their lives. In their view the industrial and technological revolution had concentrated both immense wealth and unprecedented power in the hands of capitalists on whom the restraints of culture and popular government were weak and not effective. Aided by governments they largely controlled, so the embattled farmers believed, the new corporate America dispensed the public lands to itself, let the banks shrink the money supply, and lavished both land and money on the unregulated railroads. Blaming their rising interest rates, debt, mortgages, and "hard times" on these perversions of "rugged individualism," farmers demanded that land be freely available for users, not reserved for speculators and corporations; that money be available in abundant supply to facilitate the exchange of goods, not be controlled and limited by private banks to squeeze debtors; and that railroads operate in the interest of those who had crops to send and equipment to receive, not corporations in pursuit of profit.[91]

Informing and shaping these demands was an expanded definition of democratic government that caused the Populists both to denounce what they took to be the corruption and class-based character of the existing government and to propose democratic reforms, such as the initiative, referendum, and direct election of senators, that would give the people power to control their government. Finally, the agrarian revolt was knitted together and driven by a spirit of cooperation, born of adversity and refined by experiment. When a Kansas allianceman declared that "we are emerging from a period of intense individualism, supreme selfishness, and ungodly greed to a period of cooperative effort" he expressed the essence of the Populist creed.[92] His words must also have affirmed for Gaston his own reading and writing of the past few years and given him assurance that his commitment to the Populist revolt was right for him.

These heady ideas must have been like a spring tonic to Gaston after the winter of despair caused by the failure of the National Cooperative Company. He gave all of his characteristic energy and optimism to the new challenge, enjoying the friendship he found at the *Tribune* and in the new party. For the next two and a half years he was a central figure in the party. In the 1891 fall elections for state and local offices he spoke frequently in Polk County, of which Des Moines was the seat, served on the board of the county organization, and ran unsuccessfully for coroner. The party did poorly, but defeat did not dampen enthusiasm. No sooner were the results in than a bevy of Populist notables, including Hamlin Garland and Mary Lease, showed up to launch the 1892 national campaign on the Des Moines courthouse steps. Meanwhile, Clara bore the Gastons' third child at the end of October, a boy they named Cornelius Alonzo.[93]

The following February Gaston accompanied Weaver to St. Louis for the meeting at which the party would write a platform and set the date for a convention to choose a presidential candidate. As the two men began their train journey, Gaston reflected on "the homes of the wealthy crowning the hilltops of our beautiful city." But soon, he wrote, "we were amidst the wretched hovels, which in every city mark the abode of poverty." The visible contrast of wealth and poverty reminded him forcibly of the enigma he had been struggling to understand—and do something about—since he formed his Investigating Club over two years previous. Now, he believed, he was on an odyssey during which answers would become apparent. He was hardly alone in this belief. The scene in the Exposition Music Hall, as described by an alliance reporter, must have been dazzling. He found "banners of the different states . . . fluttering like flags over an army encamped. The great stage . . . was filled with the leaders of the Alliance, the Knights of Labor, the single tax people, the Prohibitionists, the Anti-Monopolists, the People's party, the Reform Press, and the Women's Alliance." A great "feast of oratory," as one historian calls it, was climaxed by Ignatius Donnelly's "unique and startling" litany of insurgents' beliefs. Gaston knew them all, but Donnelly's rhetorical genius electrified the audience. "We meet in the midst of a nation brought to the verge of moral, political, and material ruin," he began.

> Corruption dominates the ballot-box, the Legislatures, the Congress, and touches even the ermine of the bench. The people are demoralized. . . . The newspapers are largely subsidized or muzzled, public opinion silenced, business prostrated, homes covered with mortgages, labor impoverished, and the land concentrating in the hands of the capitalists. . . . The fruits of the toil of millions are boldly stolen to build up colossal fortunes for a few, unprecedented in the history of mankind; and the possessors of those, in turn, despise the Republic and endanger liberty. From the same prolific womb of governmental injustice we breed the two great classes—tramps and millionaires.[94]

Gaston was moved by the oratory and felt privileged to meet so many leaders of the insurgency. He was particularly impressed, he wrote, "by a galaxy of noble women, the peers in ability of any men." He also must have enjoyed the singing, of which there always was a good deal at such gatherings. A *Tribune* colleague reportedly "brought down the house" with a whistling performance after which Gaston came on the stage to join him in singing an emerging favorite, "Good-Bye, My Party, Good-Bye." He returned to Des Moines to write a long account for the *Tribune,* and to enter fully into Populist Party politics. That summer, at the Omaha Convention, Weaver became the party choice for president. Gaston then took over as editor of the paper while the General carried the Populist message to the country.[95]

Gaston renewed his acquaintance with Garland in St. Louis and wrote of the creative role the writer had played in the convention. Along with Jerry Simpson, the most prominently declared single-taxer in the Party, Garland lobbied to change the language of the land plank in the platform to bring it more into line with single-tax principles. Previous declarations on the land question had called for the abolition of "alien ownership" and for the confiscation of lands held by railroads and other corporations "in excess of their actual needs." Garland and Simpson could not persuade their fellow Populists to adopt the Georgist demand that land be common property, but a clause was added that defined land as "including all the natural sources of wealth" and declared it to be "the heritage of the people." Approved in St. Louis, this language was incorporated in the Omaha platform.[96]

The 1892 presidential campaign stirred deep emotions in Americans. Weaver's oratory and apocalyptic message won some converts and impressed many others who were not prepared to say good-bye to their parties. Many responded with fear, many more with disdain. Some were violently opposed. In Georgia, for example, the General met with so much hostility that he withdrew from the state. Rotten eggs were thrown at both him and his wife by what he called a "howling mob," and he feared for his safety.[97] Over a million voters (8.8 percent of those casting ballots) favored Weaver in November, enough to give him four states and twenty-two electoral votes. A dozen Populist congressmen were dispatched to Washington while Populist governors were elected in Kansas, North Dakota, and Colorado. But in Iowa the results were dismal: only 4.7 percent of the electorate voted for Weaver. He had done better in 1880. The historian of Iowa Populism tells us that Weaver had "gained in the country but lost strength in Iowa."[98]

In addition to editing the *Tribune* during the 1892 campaign, Gaston was assistant state treasurer of the party and alternate delegate to the state convention. In 1893, when his editorial duties were lighter and his experience greater, he served as treasurer and then as secretary of the state party. He also traveled with the "silver glee club," singing and speaking at fifteen meetings in three counties, and, according to the partisan report in the *Tribune*, "creating the wildest enthusiasm." Candidates for state office in the fall did slightly better than the national ticket the previous year, but still they were woefully far from election. Always an optimist, Gaston added a politician's gloss, writing in November that "while . . . our vote has not reached the figure we had hoped, . . . a careful study of the returns gives us great reason to be encouraged." Later that month the *Tribune* reported that Gaston, the "energetic secretary of the Populist state committee," had "perfected a wise and comprehensive plan looking to the complete organization of the party in every part of the state." Early in 1894 Gaston reported much progress in the formation of Populist clubs throughout the state.[99] Party work continued through the spring and summer and even into the fall of 1894. Gaston remained party secretary, found speakers for candidates, raised money to pay off debts, and helped with the organization of Populist Party clubs.[100]

But, all the while that he was apparently fully committed to the ongoing political struggle, Gaston's restless mind was moving else-where. Since August of 1893, in fact, he had been sending out feelers to prospective colonists to let them know of a new plan he had devised; he would spend the rest of the year perfecting it. And, in November, Clara gave birth to their fourth child. They named her Leah Catherine.

VI

Cooperative Individualism

IN AUGUST OF 1893 GASTON SENT OUT A BATCH OF
letters, written on the stationery of the People's Party State Central
Committee, to former correspondents interested in the National
Cooperative Company, among others.[101] "If this reaches you and you
are still interested in Cooperation," he wrote to one, "I would like to
hear from you. You will doubtless remember corresponding with me
three years ago." One recipient replied: "I gather from your letter that
your purpose is to apply to a colonization scheme the principle of the
single tax together with other economic principles which will result in
the equitable distribution of the results of the community labor of a
colony." Later in the fall Hamlin Garland urged Gaston to finish an
article for the *Arena* on communitarian experiments. "I would like to
have you show, in your very best manner, why it is that all social
experiments have started on a wrong foundation," he wrote. He wanted
Gaston to explain, using Kaweah and Topolobampo as examples, that
such efforts always failed because "there has been no clear perception of
the relation of the land question to social experiments." Now was the
time, Garland insisted, to make that relationship clear.[102]

Gaston did not write the article Garland requested—at least none by him was published in the *Arena*—but he did produce a long essay on what he called "true cooperative individualism."[103] He used what he had learned in the previous four years of immersion in social thought and political action in his search for the right balance between the claims of society and the rights of the individual. By now the truism that human beings are both competitive and cooperative had a special meaning for him. Populists "tilted strongly toward the latter," Lawrence Goodwyn writes, "but they also confronted the enduring qualities of the former. They accepted this complexity about mankind."[104] Simply to acknowledge the complexity, however, was not enough. Somewhere one had to draw fine lines, put complex truths into workable structures for a humane social order.

The starting point for Gaston was his belief that the structure of American society did not allow for a humane social order. Too much individualism, too little cooperation, had led to too many miserable lives. On the other hand, the recent history of the communitarian experiments in cooperation seemed to him to offer no satisfactory alternative. Power concentrated in the corporate whole over too many human activities tended to run roughshod over individual differences. He agreed with one of the early historians of communitarianism that "if private property gives rise to conflict, so does community of property, and even more frequently."[105] The sad, and ironic, result was that most cooperative colonies not only undermined individualism; they also destroyed the sense of community that was their *raison d'être*. Somehow, Gaston now reasoned, individualism must be fostered within a framework of cooperation and cooperation must emerge from the self-interest in the hearts and wills of free individuals. "Cooperative individualism," a term he seems to have contributed to the lexicon of social

HEADQUARTERS
State Central Committee.

S. C. SCOTT, J. BELLANGEE,
CHAIRMAN. SECRETARY.

HOMES FOR THE TOILERS

PEOPLE'S PARTY

We want more money, and no inter-
ference by England through Wall St
with our American Financial Policy.

Des Moines, Iowa, *Aug 20* 1893

Wm Haanum
Owatonna Minn —

If this reaches you and you are
still interested in Cooperation I would
like to hear from you. You will
doubtless remember corresponding with
me three years ago.

Fraternally your
Ernest B Gaston

Seattle Wash 9/1. 93.

Dear Sir!
Above did reach me this morning, + I am still
interested in Cooperation. How did your scheme come out?
Hope you succeeded + have quite a colony by this time.
If you have any pamphlets + statements in regard to it,
please send me copy. I am not a people party man

**Gaston begins new attempt to start a colony, writing on Populist
Party stationery.**

reconstruction, was the name he gave to his new plan.[106]

Henry George's single tax was the new ingredient he felt would enable him to strike the right balance. According to James Bellangee's daughter, Anna Bellangee Call, her father brought Gaston around to the single tax. More than a half-century after Fairhope was founded, she recalled that a Des Moines single taxer named William Morphy had called her father's attention to Henry George and that he then "got Mr. E. B. Gaston and Mr. James Hunnell . . . much interested and, among that group and their friends, the idea of a demonstration of the [single-tax] theory was born." Bellangee himself wrote in 1913 that, in response to Gaston's invitation to support the National Cooperative Company venture, he had proposed a single-tax colony instead and that "subsequently we joined with others in elaborating the plan of Fairhope." Paul and Blanche Alyea, authors of an authoritative history of Fairhope published in 1956, relied on these two sources to conclude that "the single tax features of the Fairhope plan flowed from Morphy to Bellangee to Gaston."[107] Such a simple, linear description overlooks the fact that Gaston had studied George carefully at least as early as the winter of 1889 when he formed the Investigating Club. At that time he built on George's insights without accepting them as an exclusive guide. Now, over the summer of 1893, he was shifting his emphasis. There is nothing in the contemporary evidence, however, to support the claim that he was converted to George by Bellangee. Instead, the intellectual journey he began four years earlier had already exposed him to numerous influences.

Bellangee was certainly one of the important influences in his life. Seventeen years Gaston's senior, he was born on March 14, 1844, in Dover, Illinois. His father was a New Hampshire-born Quaker and horticulturist. Bellangee taught school for a brief period before he went to the University of Michigan to study four years for a science degree. After another stint as a school teacher he moved to the University of Illinois where he taught architectural and mechanical drawing from 1869-73. Then came two years as mathematics professor at the Nebraska State Normal School where he apparently acquired the title of professor with which he was thereafter addressed. He married Hattie Jameson in Illinois; their only child, Anna, was born in Nebraska in 1874. He turned to architecture for a short period before poor health and worsening eyesight led him to horticulture, the occupation he followed in Des Moines. There he built extensive greenhouses in which he cultivated winter vegetables by artificial heat and excelled in the growing of hot-house roses. His wife died in the fall of 1893, just as the plans for a new colony venture were being perfected, leaving him a forty-nine-year-old widower living with his nineteen-year-old daughter.[108]

Bellangee was well known in Des Moines as a reform activist. In 1887 he was chairman of the Greenback Party state committee; in 1891 he was president of the Des Moines Single Tax Club, founded in February of that year. The club's principles were summed up in two sentences: "We favor raising all public revenue by taxation of land values. We hold that every business in its nature a monopoly should be owned by the government." He helped form the Iowa Populist Party, was a close friend of both Weaver and Gillette, and held top offices in the party. He wrote and spoke frequently, editing for a short while in 1889 a paper called *The Opinion Outlook.* He and Gaston were close colleagues, working together intimately. "Bro. Bellangee is a deep thinker," Gaston said of his older friend, "a scholarly writer and a forcible speaker. He will waste no time, . . . but will proclaim the unadulterated doctrine of economic justice."[109]

That "unadulterated doctrine of economic justice" contained large doses of Henry George, but to many single taxers who opposed the Populist Party because of its "patchwork" platform and its presumed bent toward socialism it was an adulterated version. Stressing their commitment to individualism, strict single taxers tended to play down the very parts of George's doctrine that Bellangee and now, in 1893, Gaston emphasized. What brought Gaston so decisively to George was the shared emphasis on cooperation—on an individualist route to the cooperative commonwealth. There was plenty in George's writing to appeal to him. It was not only that George favored government owner-ship of natural monopolies, such as the railroad, the telegraph, and the telephone. More important was his vision of a cooperative society. "The natural progress of social development is unmistakably toward cooperation," he wrote in *Social Problems*. Earlier, in *Progress and Poverty*, he predicted that his reform would, on the one hand, make it possible to abolish government, "as a directing and repressive power," and, on the other, enlarge its beneficent functions. With the revenue provided by the single tax, he said,

> we could establish public baths, museums, libraries, gardens, lecture rooms, music and dancing halls, theaters, universities, technical schools, shooting galleries, play grounds, gymnasi-ums, etc. Heat, light, and motive power, as well as water, might be conducted through our streets at public expense; our roads be lined with fruit trees; discoverers and inventors rewarded, scien-tific investigations supported; and in a thousand ways the public

revenues made to foster efforts for the public benefit. We should reach the ideal of the socialist, but not through government repression. Government would change its character, and would become the administration of a great co-operative society.[110]

Gaston now built on George's thought, which he fused with Populist doctrine and a few holdover ideas from his earlier foray into community building, to define "true cooperative individualism" and explain how it could create a model community that would furnish all those benefits described in George's soaring prose.[111]

Land was central to the plan, its ownership by the community as a whole the fulcrum on which everything turned. All material progress, Georgists believed, placed increasing demands on a fixed supply of land, forcing its value up. Society as a whole created land's value, but, under the existing system, all of the increased rent—that share of income attributable solely to possession of the land—was appropriated by landowners, to the disadvantage of labor and capital. This was indefensible on both moral and economic grounds—morally because it gave to individuals something they had not earned, economically because it was the fundamental source of poverty, the explanation of the paradoxical union of progress and poverty.

The solution was to confiscate the full rental value of land through taxation, in order to give to the community that which it had created and to leave to individuals that which they created. The "law of equal freedom" would work in the community, Gaston wrote, when all members paid into the common treasury an annual rental, or "single tax," reflective of the value of the land occupied. Land would thus be free and abundantly available to all; speculators who held land out of use would never gain a foothold; and the rising demand for land in a prosperous community would provide growing revenues to make the community a model for the world. Finally, the concept of land as common property meant that scarce resources, such as waterfront property and natural wonders, would never be used for private gain or pleasure but would instead be reserved for the whole of society.

Making the land common property was the basic reform, the "cooperative" framework within which both voluntary cooperation and individual initiative would flourish. But several other "cooperative" features were outlined in Gaston's proposal. Public utilities—light, power, water, and heat—were to be operated for the "comfort and convenience of the members" and not for "pecuniary profit." Insurance for the members would also be a public, not a private, enterprise. Finally, schools, libraries, parks, baths, and places of public assembly would be the business of the whole community, not private enterprise. Gaston promised to bring to everyone in the model community "all those conveniencies—even necessities—of modern civilization which are now denied entirely to our rural population, and are so expensive that they can be afforded by a very few, comparatively, in the cities."

All of this was good Georgist doctrine. Populist influence showed through in the financial section of the essay where the "money monopoly" was decried. (Because there was no plan for a railroad, the essay was silent on the railroad monopoly.)[112] Gaston adopted good Populist rhetoric in blasting the national government for its spawning of a financial system that had become "one of the chief instruments for the virtual enslavement of the many by the few." The guarantee of a "safe, adequate and independent medium of exchange" in the new colony, Gaston believed, would be "one of the most valuable features of our enterprise." To accomplish this he proposed that the association issue scrip to be used in all financial exchanges within the community.

The final cooperative dimension of his plan was a holdover from the old days and suggests just how hard it was for him to give up on some of his socialist convictions, now reinforced by the Populist experience with cooperative merchandising. In a long section on "commercial features"—in fact, it was the longest part of the essay—Gaston analyzed the meaning of competition and then drew a sharp line between production and distribution, the "two great departments of human activity." These two activities, he insisted, rested on entirely different bases. "It has been said that competition is war, and all war is destructive," he wrote, "but this is not true." War of "individual against individual and nation against nation" was destructive, whereas "the conflicts of individuals against the forces of nature are not destructive, but productive."

Competition in production, he argued, fell in the category of "conflicts of individuals against the forces of nature" and was beneficial. It encouraged individual initiative, increased output, caused prices to drop, set wages in a free and fair market, and assured the greatest possible opportunities for meeting society's material needs. Here he was a full free-enterprise individualist, although he held out the possibility that the colony might, under special circumstances, undertake productive enterprises on its own. Competition in distribution was another matter. This was war of "individual against individual." He could find nothing to recommend it. Merchants competing with each other to sell manufactured goods and farm products caused "wasteful duplication of effort." Competition here added nothing to the stock of material goods and only provided strife among those wanting to distribute what was already available. The logical solution was cooperative merchandising—a solution the colony would apply through the creation of one or more company stores.

Having made the case for communal distribution, Gaston's Georgist individualism now supplied a crucial qualification: the colony would run its own store but any individual had the "undeniable right" to compete with it. There was to be none of the coercion he believed had undone so many of the experiments in communitarian socialism. This restraint, and the encouragement of individual differences and initiatives, was to be the hallmark of the new venture. The company, he wrote,

> does not propose to control ALL the activities of its members; to say what each shall do and what compensation he shall receive for doing it. It does not propose to interfere in any way with the religious beliefs and practices or social intercourse of individuals—to dictate what kinds of houses they shall build or what style of clothes they shall wear; to whom they shall sell or of whom they shall buy.

Colony government was to be "a pure democracy" in which "persons will rule instead of property." All adult members, "without regard to sex," were to have "equal voice" in its affairs. Individual differences would receive full expression; no one would be powerless. Elections of officers were to be frequent and terms of office short. The initiative and referendum would make it possible for all members, whether part of the governing board or not, to introduce legislation and bring controversial issues to a popular vote; and salaries of officers were to be modest, never an inducement to office holding.

"We have sought to build for humanity as it is," Gaston claimed, again distinguishing his effort from that of such places as Kaweah and Topolobampo. His plans were offered "not as the views of a dreamer but as a practical business proposition to practical men and women; not as plans requiring . . . qualities properly supposed to belong to angels, . . . but the result of joint efforts of many, agreed on fundamental economic principles, to apply them in harmony with the known and constant springs of human action." He closed out his essay with a glowing description of the possibilities and an appeal to his fellow reformers: "In such an effort we invite the co-operation of all of kindred aims."

Gaston showed the essay to his friends in the fall and early winter of 1893; their warm response, along with the encouraging replies to his August inquiries, led to the gathering in his office on January 4, 1894, when he read the paper to twelve fellow Populists. At the end of the meeting they voted unanimously to put his ideas "into practical operation at once." Gaston and four of his colleagues—Bellangee, L. R. Clements, Alf Wooster, and J. P. Hunnell—were assigned the task of drawing up a constitution.[113] They finished their work quickly and presented it to the whole group on January 31. At this meeting the name Fairhope Industrial Association was adopted, the constitution approved, and officers chosen. The name "Fairhope" was suggested by Alf Wooster, who remarked that they had a "fair hope" of success.[114]

The term "industrial association" evoked then, as it does not now, close ties to the complex world of pre-Civil War utopian socialism and communitarian reform as well as to post-bellum radicalism. Saint-Simon used the term *industriel* in the first part of the nineteenth century and linked it to social reform. The American followers of Fourier often characterized their philosophy as "the doctrine of Industrial Association." In their lexicon industrial associations were the phalanxes, or small model communities, designed to show how the larger society should be restructured.[115] In the 1880s and 1890s the term industrial organizations was used by radicals of various sorts, including Populists, to describe collections of working people or, sometimes, the dispossessed. Thus, the name the Fairhopers chose linked them to a broad tradition of utopian socialism and indigenous radicalism rather than to the specific single-tax reform.[116]

In mid-February the *Tribune* announced the creation of the Fairhope Industrial Association and explained that it had "been organized by a number of leading Populists of this state and others to make a practical demonstration of the soundness and beneficence of the principles we have been advocating as a party." The same connection was made by other newspapers as well as by prospective colonists. And when H. C. Nixon came to write the history of the Iowa party in 1924, he simply recorded what he must have taken as conventional wisdom: the Fairhope Industrial Association was created, he wrote, "to put into operation the reform demands of the People's Party."[117]

So bald an identification of the Fairhope plan with the "reform demands of the People's Party" overlooks the uniquely important role of the single tax in the colony plan and masks a fundamental difference between Georgists and most Populists regarding land. Georgists believed it should be common property; most Populists believed it should be private property. Nixon also ignores Fairhoper dissent from some of the Populists' demands, especially their advocacy of a graduated income tax. Nonetheless, Fairhope was a product of the Populist Revolt.

It was inspired by the Populist vision of a democratic society, shaped by the Populist experience, and created by Populist Party members.

All of those present at the January 4 meeting were Populist Party members, as were the twelve officers chosen on January 31.[118] Among them were some of the best-known leaders of Iowa populism. Edward A. Ott, chosen vice-president, was a young minister, not yet thirty, a faculty member at Drake who had been a candidate for Congress in 1892.[119] James Sovereign, prominent in both the Greenback and Populist parties, served as state commissioner of labor statistics and became head of the Knights of Labor in 1893, succeeding Terence V. Powderly.[120] Alf Wooster, the man who thought up the name Fairhope, served with Gaston on the *Tribune* editorial staff and edited *Liberty Bell*, the official organ of the colony for a while; he succeeded Gaston as secretary of the state party.[121] Others included George B. Lang, lecturer and state organizer for the Southern Alliance in Iowa; S. S. Mann, an executive committee member of the Alliance; and T. E. Mann, a "presiding judge" of the Knights of Labor, mayor of Gladbrook, Iowa, and a nominee for Congress from the 5th district.[122]

The constitution adopted by these Populist single-taxers declared that the purpose of their Fairhope Industrial Association was

> to establish and conduct a model community or colony, free from all forms of private monopoly, and to secure to its members therein, equality of opportunity, the full reward of individual efforts, and the benefits of co-operation in matters of general concern.[123]

In precise detail, the constitution made concrete the principles described in Gaston's essay—democratic government; free enterprise in production, cooperation in distribution; community control of public utilities; an adequate money supply; and complete freedom in personal and religious activities. Membership was open to anyone over eighteen at a cost of two hundred dollars, the terms of payment to be determined by the executive council. An additional one hundred dollars might be assessed to stock the company store. No test of fidelity to principles was stipulated, but the executive council had to approve all applications and any person winning its endorsement could be rejected by a petition signed by ten percent of the membership.

The article on land revealed how the single tax would provide the basic framework for the community, making possible the balance between cooperation and individualism. Private ownership of land was prohibited. All land belonged to the association "as trustee for its entire membership." Long-term leases issued to members carried with them "full and absolute right to the use and control of lands . . . and to the ownership and disposition of all improvements made or products produced thereon." Each member was required to pay to the association an annual rental based on the executive council's appraised value of the land irrespective of improvements on it. The association would pay all county and state taxes on the land and improvements within the community. Thus, the only tax the members would pay would be the tax on land values; in this way, the workings of George's single-tax reform would be demonstrated.

With the rent determined according to the value of the land only, the Fairhopers believed there would be every incentive to maximize its use and complete freedom from the penalties upon individual enterprise of the existing system of taxation. Free land, they believed, would mean free people. Communal responsibility for collecting and disbursing land rents would nurture a sense of community and encourage cooperative ventures. Community life would be laid on an ethical basis, incorporating General Weaver's aphorism, soon to be on the masthead of the association newspaper: "That which Nature provides is the Common Property of all God's Children; that which the Individual creates belongs to the Individual; that which the Community creates belongs to the Community."[124]

VII

Place and People

W. E. BROKAW, EDITOR OF THE ST. LOUIS *SINGLE Tax Courier*, wrote to Gaston on January 23, 1894, to praise the Cooperative Individualism essay. The distinction between competition in production and cooperation in distribution was new to him but he liked it. "The fact that all your provisions look to securing members freedom to cooperate *or not* and to securing the *primary* & *essential* of freedom—equal freedom in the use of the earth— makes me feel that such a colony *ought*, at least, prosper better than any other cooperative colonies yet started." In a postscript he added, "Send a paper to E. Q. Norton, Daphne, Baldwin Co., Ala. & ask him about price of land in that Co., & about advantages & disadvantages there for such a colony as yours. He & wife are great s-trs."[125] Brokaw's letter pointed to the principal tasks Gaston and his colleagues now faced—to broadcast news of the colony beyond the group of people with whom Gaston had personally corresponded, to acquaint them with its novel features; to recruit as large a membership as possible; and, to choose a site so that definite plans for moving could be laid.

The first task was the easiest. The Reform Press Association, a creation of the Populist movement, spread the news through cooperat-

INCORPORATED 1894 · · · AUTHORIZED CAPITAL, $1,000,000.00 · · · SHARES, $200.00

FAIRHOPE
INDUSTRIAL ASSOCIATION

Organized for the Practical Application of Economic Truth
Co-operation in Matters of General Concern. · Absolute Freedom in Individual Affairs.

Des Moines, Iowa, 6/6 1894.

Dear Wooster —

I wish you would mail to enclosed list copies of this works and May 19th Bells and send me 30 or 40 new copies of 19th if you have them with this works. I am getting lots of new inquiries. Whoop up the Institution.

Hastily,

E. B. Gaston

A hurried note from E.B. Gaston to Alf Wooster, on the stationery of Fairhope Industrial Association.

ing newspapers across the country. Wooster, who was secretary of the Iowa Reform Press Association, left the *Tribune* to devote full time to the *Liberty Bell*, a paper he had owned since the end of 1890. It became the official organ of the Fairhope Industrial Association with copies going to all prospective members. At the end of April the *Bell* reported that secretary Gaston had enthusiastic inquiries from all parts of the United States and several foreign countries. But it was going to take much "missionary work," Wooster wrote to Gaston, "to get people to understand the difference between our plan and the 'regulation' cooperative move."[126] No one understood better than Gaston how much "missionary work" was required and he plunged into it with his customary energy and optimism.

Meanwhile, he knew his work would be eased by the early selection of a site; he was reported in the April 28 *Liberty Bell* to be "securing all the reliable information he can upon the advantages and disadvantages of various sections of the country and a committee . . . will be sent out soon to make thorough personal investigations." Wooster wrote stressing how important it was that interested persons sign up. The larger the membership, the better the chances of reduced fares to the colony site. The membership fee was cut to $175 for those applying before May 15 and it could be paid in monthly installments of five dollars. Suggestions for likely sites poured into Des Moines, some from personal acquaintances, some from real estate agents, some from newly interested communitarians. At the May 11 meeting of the Executive Council, Bellangee and S. S. Mann, two of the older members of the association, were chosen to investigate possible sites. They were off soon for an inspection tour in six southern states.[127]

There is little direct evidence to explain why the search was restricted to the South. Two powerful factors certainly were climate and cost. Iowa winters were not easy to live through and the summer heat in Des Moines was often oppressive; land prices in the South were low, a strong attraction for a group as impecunious as the Fairhopers were likely to be. Most communitarian experiments of the 1880s and early 1890s had been located west of Iowa, in the Plains and Rocky Mountain states or the Pacific coast. Few experimental communities, up to this time, had been planted in the South.[128] The Pacific coast was far away and even an exploratory visit would have been too expensive; the

Plains and Rocky Mountain states were as cold as Iowa. The strong ties of the Iowa Populists to the Southern Alliance may well have been another another factor. In one of his early contributions as managing editor of the *Tribune*, Gaston had written that "the intelligent citizens of Alabama are in the People's Party."[129]

Climate, cost, and fraternal ties directed the Iowa Populists' search southward, but that decision did not stir them to try to liberate the region's former slaves from the exploitation they suffered at the hands of a white supremacist South. This was hardly surprising, since racial justice was almost never among the causes championed by communitarian reformers, wherever located. Frederick Douglass, writing of the antebellum Northampton Association, said that "men and women who were interested in the emancipation of civilization were also deeply interested in the emancipation of slaves"; but that interest, probably not as extensive as Douglass believed, did not emerge in a programmed commitment to racial equality after emancipation.[130] The socialist followers of J. A. Wayland, for example, established their whites-only colony in Ruskin, Tennessee, just a few months before the Fairhopers set out for Alabama, with nothing in their socialist ideology opening their eyes to the racism around them.[131]

Radicals generally in late nineteenth century America had little understanding of or involvement in southern racial matters, and erstwhile abolitionists continued steadily retreating from their earlier commitment.[132] Among white Americans, ironically, the southern Populists were the ones who had moved most boldly to understand the deeper meaning and cruel penalties of racial division and hierarchy, but their will to challenge the received culture—marked by dramatic displays of interracial solidarity, especially in the 1892 election—was neither universal among their members nor long sustainable against charges of racial treason.[133] Gaston had sympathized with their courage and their achievement, writing in 1892 that "the Alabama election has knocked out what little life there was remaining in the negro domination cry in the South." He reminded his readers of the cry of "Negro Domination" that Democrats hurled at Alliancemen "who dared to defy their corrupt and despotic management," and he praised them for having won "by the aid of the negro vote."[134]

Negroes had more than their vote to offer progressive men and women like the Fairhopers. At the famous Ocala meeting of the Farmers' Alliance in December 1890, the southern black farmers, meeting separately from the whites, declared that "land belongs to the sovereign people" and unanimously adopted a resolution favoring the single-tax. As Ronald Yanosky points out, their declaration challenged the widespread belief that blacks could solve their economic problems solely by "sacrifice, hard work, and careful management." It also set them apart from their white brethren, and marked them as true radicals when, as Yanosky writes, they argued for "a structural reform in property relations . . . which would offer productive resources on equal terms to white and black." It was the wisdom of precisely this "structural reform" that the Fairhopers were setting out to demonstrate. They were to do so, however, without allying themselves with African Americans or their cause. No urging to do differently came from the national single-tax movement. "I am afraid of this race question," George wrote privately in 1890, fearing the sectional antagonism it could arouse. His newspaper found the single-tax declaration of the black farmers "amusing," and made no effort to respond to their initiative.[135]

Henry George wrote very little about racism in *Progress and Poverty* or in his other books, but he frequently described the private ownership of land and of human beings as moral equivalents; each permitted unconscionable control of one person over another. More germane to the post-war situation, he wrote that planters "sustained no loss" owing to emancipation because they owned the land on which the freedman had no choice but to work. They received, in fact, "a greater proportionate share of the earnings of their laborers than they did under the system of chattel slavery, and the laborers a less share."[136]

Both Gaston and Bellangee accepted this analysis. It informed Gaston's subsequent arguments about how the single tax would help eliminate southern sharecropping, and it shaped the reports Bellangee dispatched to his Iowa associates on the southern racial situation.[137] He found the blacks he met in the South to be less lively and self-confident in their behavior than those back home. "In their manners they seem to be thoroughly cowed. They fully realize that they are 'niggers.'" The explanation lay in white behavior, not black character:

> The white people seem to regard it as an essential that the negroes should be kept down and they are most effectually doing it, but that the removal of the repression would be quickly followed by a rise of the negro ambition is evidenced by the avidity and buoyancy with which they avail themselves of any courtesies or show of equality that are extended to them by the whites. This is urged by the native whites as proof positive of the necessity of treating them as inferiors, but to my mind it is the most pathetic evidence of the injustice of the conditions under which they live that could be afforded.

Alert to at least some of the realities of southern racism, Bellangee nonetheless did not counsel making an assault on it part of the association's mission. He believed that institution of the single tax would necessarily reduce racism through improved economic circumstances. Thus, although the conditions dictated by the whites were "for the present all-controlling," the single tax would eventually transform them.

Gaston shared both Bellangee's environmentalist explanation of Negro inferiority and his belief that the antidote to it was the single tax. Responding gently in 1890 to a critic who objected to the choosing of a site in Louisiana for the National Cooperative Company, he said, "I believe the low grade of civilization found so apparent in the South is due to the curse of slavery and other causes." Economic justice was the answer.[138] To another critic, a Texas crank who loaded him up with letters in 1890 and again in 1893 demanding that Gaston's colony keep out non-Christians, blacks, and drinkers, he said he did not think it a good idea to have restrictive clauses but that members could always vote to bar objectionable people.[139]

As they traveled through the South, Bellangee and Mann paid relatively little attention to race. Instead, they focused on land prices, climate, aesthetic features, soil conditions, crop possibilities, commercial arrangements, and likely local reactions to their radical experiment.[140] They seem to have explored no possibilities for manufacturing. Bellangee wrote long letters to Gaston as well as reports that were published in *Liberty Bell*, making it possible for prospective colonists to follow the travels of their comrades and share in the excitement of visualizing where they might soon be living.

In Arkansas the two committeemen found little to attract them.

"Mr. Mann is sighing for the gulf breezes," Bellangee wrote. "He is disgusted with the stumps and stones of the hill country." Bellangee found that "the low lands, including Grand Prairie, are not healthy and the uplands are so rough and stony it will be hard to find a good place in Ark. All told I like Randolph Co. best but we can not get any such a chance there as at Grand P." Louisiana prospects seemed brighter even though the gulf breeze they yearned for was "off duty" when they reached Lake Charles, so that they "suffered a good deal with heat and mosquitoes." But the area was attractive as "a fruit country to be sure" and the rice culture was well established. They entered into serious negotiations for four thousand acres at Bayou Shere, but the cost for what they would need to become rice growers was prohibitively high. In Texas they found a large tract eighteen miles from Houston, wholly unimproved prairie and timber land, but generally they were disappointed by uncooperative real estate agents, hot weather, and the "discovery that Texan laws were not favorable to any colony scheme." The only Mississippi site they looked at was too expensive and poorly situated. Then they arrived in Baldwin County, Alabama.[141]

Gaston had followed Brokaw's advice to contact Edward Quincy Norton in Daphne, Alabama, one of the small settlements on the eastern shore of Mobile Bay. An avid single taxer, Norton and his wife hosted Mann and Bellangee for three days, showing them available sites and urging them to plant their colony in the vicinity. Bellangee wrote glowingly about what he saw:

> We viewed the land & country over the hills and along the shore. It is lovely indeed. High banks and sandy beach with every here and there a spring gushing out of the bank with

sufficient fall to raise the water by means of rams to the table lands above.

The view from the shore is magnificent. Looking across the bay about eight or ten miles Mobile lies in full view and away below between it and the gulf lies a long stretch of the western shore of the Bay. The bay is quite calm and placid at even tide and the absence of litter and sea weed and the gently sloping beach makes it a lovely place to bathe. . . .

Along the beach on the east side of the bay there are old houses formerly owned by rich people & kept for homes. Now they are in a dilapidated condition, many of them, and occupied in many instances by colored people. . . . Land back away from the bay can be bought for 50 cts to $1.00 per acre. It is covered with fine timber and is no account for farming purposes except as it is fertilized. But it lies high and is nearly level. There are fine streams for water power and with proper labor can be made very attractive and profitable.

I believe it is the healthiest region we have struck yet.

If we could secure a mile frontage on the bay and a good body of land running back to the table lands we would be nicely fixed.

To my mind the greatest drawback is the absence of a railroad on that side of the bay. To ship our products north it would be necessary to go 25 miles by land to railroad or by boat to Mobile. We would be somewhat handicapped. I would not however want to live on the Mobile side near the city.

Bellangee then added what must have been a special inducement to think favorably about this site with which he was so taken: "Henry

HYGEIA HOTEL,
Citronelle, Ala.
Dr. J. G. MICHAEL, Prop.

CITRONELLE, ALA. July 16 1894

E. B. Gaston
1350 27th St Des Moines Ia
Dear Friend: We left
Naxton's Saturday afternoon after
spending with him three days of
most pleasant and profitable
time. He is a nice man and
his wife is a very intelligent lady.
We viewed the county over
Over the hills and along the shore
It is lovely indeed. High banks
and sandy beach with every here
and there a spring gushing out

Bellangee writes of the future Fairhope site.

George was at Norton's place and was delighted with it. Norton thinks that if we go there we will be able to get George's endorsement of the project and make it a big single tax enterprise."[142] Bellangee was presumably aware of George's well-known statement opposing communitarian experiments to demonstrate the single tax. Perhaps he and Norton thought Fairhope would be the exception that would change his mind. Fairhope's historians, Paul and Blanche Alyea, are probably right to dismiss the notion as "pure wishful thinking."[143]

Before they returned to Des Moines, Bellangee and Mann visited another site in Alabama, north of Mobile, and one in western Tennessee on which they reported favorably, noting its mild temperature, generous rainfall, and suitability to such staple crops as cotton and tobacco as well as to stock raising and dairy farming. Back home, they described in detail their observations to their fellow Fairhopers and, on instructions from the executive council, prepared a lengthy report to be published, along with material already printed in *Liberty Bell*, on August 15, 1894, in the maiden issue of the association's new paper, the *Fairhope Courier*. Armed with detailed information about the various possibilities, members could then be asked to choose from among them.[144]

A year had passed since Gaston launched his new effort to found a cooperative colony. On the whole it had been a satisfying and successful time: his essay on cooperative individualism had been widely praised, by friends and strangers alike, as pointing to a unique and workable way of resolving the conflict between cooperation and individualism; Populist comrades in Des Moines had answered his call to consider a new venture; and, since then, a constitution had been drawn up, a charter secured, potential sites identified, and the association's own newspaper was about to be published. Wooster's *Liberty Bell* had served as the colony's outlet, but it was a general interest paper and members now wanted a journal of their own. The executive council voted on August 10 to launch the *Fairhope Courier*, with Gaston as editor. He was already the only paid officer, receiving since February a monthly salary of forty dollars for his position as secretary, and the only person who worked full time promoting the colony. As editor of the association's paper, he could more efficiently coordinate the final push toward creating the model community.[145] That effort would depend heavily on how many and what kinds of persons would join the association and then actually make the trip to the site they selected.

Gaston must have had a few dark moments remembering how only two men had joined his previous effort, in 1890. On the other hand, he was cheered by the many favorable responses that came to him. L. B. Baker, writing from Findlay, Ohio, said "the reformers in this locality are greatly interested in the 'buz' of the 'Co-operative bee.'" There seemed to be "widespread longing" for something like the Fairhope plan. A Topolobampo veteran wrote: "I see you have embodied the good points of the Credit Foncier Colony of Topolobampo, and omitted the bad ones in your plan and I do think it is the best I have ever seen." Another Topolobampo colonist, whose experience there he described as "disastrous," was "highly pleased" with the Fairhope plan because of its emphasis on "the freedom of the individual" in employment. To him, the Fairhope plan had "the seasoning of common sense which is so sadly lacking in most co-operative enterprises." One Populist who had a low opinion of the single tax liked the Fairhope plan nonetheless: "I don't approve of the single tax theory, but if it dont work right you can correct it. We will not divide on that account." George

FAIRHOPE COURIER.

That which Nature provides is the Common Property of all God's Children; that which the Individual creates belongs to
the Individual; that which the Community creates belongs to the Community. —GRⁿ ⸱ ᵂᴱᴬᵛᴱᴿ.

VOL. I. DES MOINES, IOWA, AUGUST 15, 1894. NO. 1.

THROUGH THE SOUTH.

**The Fairhope Locating Committee Renders Its
Final Report.**

DES MOINES, IA., *Aug. 9, 1894.*
To the Members of Fairhope Industrial Association,

Gentlemen:
Your committee to whom was referred the
matter of location of the future home of the Association,
beg leave to submit the following report:

Your committee is mindful of the fact that the natural
limitations in perception and judgment combined with
the bias of individual tastes and prejudices renders it an
exceedingly difficult task for them to choose for all of the
members of the Association, the location which would best
suit each and every one. Even were they to choose for
emselves alone, the task is not without grave difficulties
each locality visited has its special advantages and
advantages, so varying in degree and so unlike in char-
er as to scarcely be susceptible of classification or
comparison. They therefore feel that they can best serve
the Association by setting forth to its members the characteristic features of the various localities visited, leaving
the members entirely free to choose without recommen-
dation from the committee.

Your committee endeavored to embody in their letters
to *Liberty Bell* much of the detailed description of places
which they visited and they desire that those letters, or
consider a supplemental part of this report.

In most situations examined by us enough land can be
secured in a body to answer the purposes of the Association

things that he can eat, he will raise only enough to feed
himself and the land-lord receives nothing for his rent.
Thence for the most part he is required to raise cotton or
tobacco or some crop that he cannot eat and that brings a
sure price (however small) in the market. Again, the negro seldom becomes an owner of land and owing to the
constant decline of cotton in the market, his cultivation
of the soil as a renter brings constantly less and less returns
to the land owner and as a result the price of lands in the
negro sections is falling rather than rising. There is also
a disinclination to sell to negroes. The dislike of a northern man to settle alone in a negro neighborhood makes it
difficult for the owners of lands to sell them, hence we
found prices of lands in neighborhoods where northerners
had got a footing, higher than in sections where negroes
predominated.

In the prairie lands of the south the chief occupation has
been grazing with the result that successful stock raisers
have secured large tracts of land and held them uncultivat-
ed thereby retarding the growth of the country. This is
the case in many sections of Texas.

The development of the railroad interests of the south
and especially the opening up of north and south lines has
induced in the southern states the industry of "truck farming." With practically the whole year in which to grow
vegetables, the extreme south is able to supply the tables
of the north with an abundance of them at seasons of the
year when they are delicacies and command a high price.
In this industry the extreme south has the advantage of
the intermediate sections, the difference in freights being
more than counterbalanced by the gain in the season.
As feed for stock can be grown at any season in the south

The Fairhope Courier, volume 1, number 1.

89

Pollay, a single taxer and a future member, wrote from California to say the plan was the best he had ever seen. "I am sure it will be acceptable to any honest reformer whether as a worker in the ranks of the S.T. '(single eye *socialist)*' or in the ranks of the full fledged '*socialist*.'" Gilbert Anderson, a future member from St. Louis, wrote to say he had "contemplated for some months" joining a cooperative colony but, until he saw the Fairhope plan, was discouraged by the "curtailment of individual liberties in communities as generally managed; this would be largely avoided under the Fairhope Constitution." And from England the organizer of a Bellamy-type thoroughly socialist colony thanked Gaston for his criticism of his group's constitution and remarked that "certainly your plan is simpler, more businesslike, and better suited to human nature as we now know it."[146]

While Gaston furnished the reform community of America with brochures Bellangee urged him to guard against admitting the wrong kinds of persons. Just after leaving the Baldwin County site, irritated by a seemingly errant remark by Mann, he wrote: "Gaston, I am more than ever convinced that we must take great pains to get single taxers only into it. Otherwise we will wreck the thing by dissension."[147] The membership application form asked what "trade or reform organizations" applicants had been members of and what works "on sociology or economics" they had read. They had to "fully approve of the principles" set forth in the constitution, but the single tax was not mentioned specifically.[148] As it turned out, no apparent effort was made to determine the single-tax leanings of applicants, apart from what was volunteered in the exchange of letters between them and secretary Gaston, and no application for membership was denied. The real problem, as Gaston understood only too well, was to get members in sufficient numbers to sign up, not to probe too deeply into the particulars of their reform impulse.

Bellangee's wish for a colony of single taxers would have been easier to realize if the national single tax leaders had supported Fairhope. But they did not. "I am afraid you cannot rely on Mr. George as an ally," one supporter wrote to Gaston, "unless his opinions have undergone a change." His opinions, which had not undergone a change, were most prominently expressed in his paper, *The Standard*, in 1889. A "single tax city" would not work and should not be encouraged, he wrote, because "the single tax cannot be fairly tried on a small scale in a community not subject to the single tax." Years later, in 1917, the prominent single taxer Fiske Warren claimed that George had been asked specifically about Fairhope and that his judgment was "unfavorable." According to Warren, George "held it was not advisable to risk the reputation of the Single Tax on the success of a pioneering experiment in land, which might fail for practical reasons entirely unconnected with the principle." He also objected to Fairhope, at least according to Warren, because it "seemed to him more akin to the nationalization of land than to the Single Tax."[149]

Many single taxers were less concerned about either the chances of failure or the fine points of the method of application. For them, the real problem was that the Fairhope plan smacked too much of socialism. Even William Morphy, the man allegedly responsible for getting the single-tax idea to the forefront, remained aloof because he objected to what he saw as a "determination to experiment with artificial cooperation." George White, urging Gaston to enlist as many "straight" single taxers as possible, warned him that "what single taxers here seem to be afraid of is . . . that socialism will prevail and the resulting dissensions break up the colony." Bolton Hall, a prominent single taxer who would later change his mind about Fairhope, wrote early in 1894 to criticize the cooperative features of the plan, especially the cooperative store. He recited standard Georgist arguments against colonial experiments and added still another objection: Georgists should devote all of their energy to political campaigns for the single tax. A San Francisco single taxer, among many others, made the same point. "Before your colony will have time to bear fruit," James S. Reynolds wrote, "we shall have, under local option laws, our principle well under way in more than one city or county and possibly state, without being obliged to buy the land and to wait for a new community to create land values. . . . It is coming soon, and we want your help to bring it. I fear your energy will be largely wasted on the colony plan."[150]

Jerry Simpson—the single-taxer "Socrates of the Prairies" and Populist Congressman from Kansas—had a different view of reform through politics. He put it bluntly to Gaston: "it is my opinion that there is no possibility of getting any reform measures whatever through this Congress." In addition to questioning the political process, many single taxers found the Fairhope plan attractive. "I have never had much faith in co-operation," Perry Pepoon confessed, "but your constitution is so framed as to appeal to one's common sense, and, having the right kind of people in charge, it may gain the right kind of recruits." Clarence Moore, who would shortly become a member, wrote to say that he was "sorry that you have not the endorsement of Henry George, or Tom Johnson or James Maguire or some one of that sort." But then he added: "I was pleased to notice Hamlin Garland's letter." Gaston was, too. His friend had "given us much encouragement," he wrote, and then printed Garland's glowing endorsement:

I'd like to say a word about Brother E. B. Gaston's Fairhope colony. It is, so far as I can see, a perfect application of single-tax individualism. It is wondrously well thought out. A splendid speech or series of them could be based on the little prospectus he issues. I hope single-tax men will support Brother Gaston to the full extent of their means, and build a practicable working model of the social group we hope to see the whole nation become.[151]

Garland was a steadfast friend, a prominent writer and single taxer whose support Gaston especially valued. Earlier in the summer he told Gaston: "I have never believed in a colony—even a single-tax colony—because I believe we should work to make the whole nation a 'Fair-hope' colony." But he had changed his mind because he believed Gaston's was "the first reasonable clear-sighted and practicable plan for a colony" he had ever seen and Gaston's "most able primer of principles" had aroused his enthusiasm.[152] Garland's endorsement and the support of the *Single Tax Courier* were helpful but the national single-tax movement remained aloof. To its leaders Fairhope was on the periphery; it was not of their making and it lacked the kind of philosophical unity and simplicity that gave their movement its special sense of mission—a mission Gaston and his associates did not appear to them to be part of.[153] Fairhopers were thus cut off from crucial resources they believed they needed to succeed.

To make matters more difficult, many traditional communitarian reformers—those accustomed to what Wooster called the "'regulation' cooperative move"—were suspicious of the Fairhope tilt toward individualism. These people were inclined to look elsewhere to fulfill their reformist hopes. No more telling evidence of this can be found than in contrasting the recruiting success of the Ruskin colony with Fairhope's. A thoroughly "regulation" cooperative venture, Ruskin was the brain-child of J. A. Wayland, whose socialist paper *The Coming Nation* had a circulation of nearly 100,000. Established in Tennessee in the summer of 1894, Ruskin attracted more than four times as many people as Fairhope, even with a membership fee of five hundred dollars. Most of its members were displaced New England garment and mill workers. 154

Gaston's response to finding himself in the middle of contentious individualists and cooperators was to hold fast to the new middle ground he believed he had discovered. In mid September he reported signing up a new member who "understands our plans thoroughly and is sound on all the counts—land, money, voluntary co-operation." With the *Courier* now in his hands he would persuade all factions that "cooperative individualism" offered a workable solution to America's problems—and the best formula for the creation of a small model community. In the paper's first issue he contrasted Fairhope with Ruskin, condemned compulsory cooperative manufacturing, and passed this advice on to prospective members:

> If you value freedom and want to "hoe your own row" with a fair field and no favors—co-operating only as you feel disposed at the time—we will be glad to welcome you as a "Fairhoper." If you think it best, that all industries should be operated collec-tively, under the management of directors who shall assign the work and determine the compensation of each, you had far better join some other colony founded on that idea. 155

In the next issue, his lead article reiterated the Fairhoper faith in "self-directed labor" but made the case for co-operative production where peculiar circumstances warranted. Practical experience, not doctrinal rigidity, would be the best guide. Another essay recited the "errors of socialism," taking off from the Ruskin requirement that men work according to their abilities and be rewarded according to their needs. In a related piece on "Fairhope vs. Altruism," he argued that the Fairhope plan was unique because it was based on a realistic understanding of human nature. Unlike Ruskin and other socialist colonies its success would not require its members to abandon self-interest. He put it this way:

> In the Fairhope plans we have endeavored to establish justice, to remove the opportunities for the preying of one upon another. Recognizing that selfishness has been the ruling force of mankind from the infancy of the race, we have not been so foolish as to command or expect that it should immediately cease. Selfishness says "take," love says "give"; we may not command a gift, but we can say to him whose impulse is to take—"take that which belongs to you by right of creation, no more." This we do. We close the gates against injustice; we open them to unselfishness. Society can do no more.[156]

In more formal language, he crafted a concise statement of the purpose and character of the association. Published in the September 1 issue of the *Courier*, it was his final attempt, before setting off, to define the middle ground he wished to stake out between the competing tugs of individualists and cooperators:

The only plan of co-operative colonization ever proposed which secures the benefits of co-operation and yet preserves the perfect freedom of Individuals.

ITS PURPOSE is to establish and maintain a model community or colony free from all forms of private monopoly and to secure to its members therein, equality of opportunity, the full reward of individual effort and the benefits of co-operation in matters of general concern.

The LAW OF EQUAL FREEDOM is the corner stone of its plan. That: "every one has freedom to do all that he wills provided he infringes not the equal freedom of any other."

IN GOVERNMENT this law is applied by PERSONAL instead of STOCK VOTE with no distinction of sex and the Initiative and Referendum:

IN LAND HOLDING AND USE by the principle of the Single-tax: the association holding the title to all lands and leasing to individuals in quantities to suit at a rental "which shall equalize the varying advantages of location and natural qualities of all tracts":

IN A MEDIUM OF EXCHANGE by the issuance of its non-interest bearing notes, for services and products, redeemable in services, products and land rents:

IN COMMERCE by association stores selling goods to members and non-members alike and dividing the profits quarterly among members in proportion to their purchases and by acting as agent for its members in the sale of products, charging only cost of service rendered:

IN NATURAL MONOPOLIES—supplying water, light,

power, telephones, transportation, etc., by association control and operation at cost.

ALL CO-OPERATION VOLUNTARY. Participation in all co-operative features is purely voluntary, all being at perfect liberty to buy or sell where they please, to use the association's medium of exchange or let it alone as they please. In short to be the absolute directors of their own actions—limited only by the law of equal freedom before enunciated.

These arguments rounded out Gaston's public appeal for members. Privately, he dispatched a heavy flow of letters to everyone who expressed even a slight interest.

The August 15 issue of the Courier carried the long report of the location committee. The issue of September 1 proudly listed a "roll of honor" of twenty-one paid-up members, and announced a forthcoming membership vote to select a site. Given all the publicity and all the work, Gaston and his colleagues had not succeeded in recruiting a large membership. The association was formed in January with nineteen men taking part in its creation, either as participants at the first meeting or as officers elected on January 31. Only ten of those nineteen men made the required payments to be members in good standing at the time the site was to be selected. Five of the additional eleven members, one of them a founder's relative, were from Iowa, three were from Ohio, and there was one each from California, Indiana, and Missouri.[157] Spouses of members were not required to pay a membership fee, but could vote if they signed the constitution. Now this small group would exercise the first democratic act of the association—casting a ballot to choose a location. Most of the members had nothing more than the reports published in *Liberty Bell* and the *Courier* to guide them. It took a large measure of faith to act on those alone.

The results of the balloting were announced in the October 1 *Courier*. Baldwin County, Alabama, was the overwhelming favorite, with twenty-six first place votes. Western Tennessee was favored by eight of the members. "We believe the decision was a wise one," Gaston commented, "and that it will meet the approval of friends of the movement throughout the country." He announced the receipt of an application from his Populist comrade, J. R. Sovereign, Master Workman of the Knights of Labor, and published a glowing endorsement from John R. Commons, a rising young professor of political economy, destined to be a major influence in that field; Commons proclaimed the Fairhope scheme "the most promising plan of co-operation which I have ever seen." With the site selected and the endorsements flowing in, Gaston launched a final push in October to enlist additional members and encourage them to be among the group of pioneer settlers which he planned to lead in mid-November.[158]

VIII

To the Promised Land

D ES MOINES FAIRHOPERS CAME IN GOOD NUMBERS to the train station on the evening of Monday, November 12, 1894. Their cheer and optimism contrasted sharply with the chill of the evening and the gray sky. It had not yet snowed but winter in Des Moines was not far away. The Fairhope vanguard was setting out none too early for a warm and agreeable setting in which to begin the demonstration of the theories that had been so carefully refined from the discussions of the previous five years. The executive council met in Iowa for the last time on October 26, to lay plans for the journey south. November 15 was set for the rendezvous in Baldwin County.

Of the many who came to the station, few had much more to offer than good wishes and godspeed in the new work. James Bellangee and S. S. Mann, the two who had found the site and written so lyrically about it, were staying behind. Bellangee, in fact, was campaigning for state auditor on the Populist ticket. Nor were President Clements, Vice President Ott, five of the six councilmen, and the three trustees going to the "promised land." Only Secretary Gaston and Councilman Hunnell among the association officers would participate in the planting of their colony. Jimmy Hunnell had sold his printing business a few weeks earlier and was already in Alabama, making arrangements for the roundup on the fifteenth and seeing to the safe arrival of the Gaston and Hunnell family possessions, including Gaston's cow and his mare, Dolly. Setting off from Des Moines for the South that evening were only Hunnell's parents, Mary, sixty-two, and John, seventy-three, neither a member of the association, and the Gaston family.[159]

In the final issues of the *Courier* printed in Des Moines, Gaston made urgent appeals for support. "Friends, your membership and your money mean more to us now than they ever will again," he wrote in the October 1 issue. "We cannot buy land or goods or make public improvements with your promises, hopes or good wishes. They encourage us but we cannot 'realize' on them." In the next issue he asked for help again—"now to help plant Fairhope on the chosen spot." And he wondered: "shall we ask in vain?"[160] He stayed up late every night writing letters to encourage doubting members to be present at the roundup. A few more applications and a few more dollars came in during October and early November in response to these pleadings and to the news of a site having been selected. Still, there was much doubt about who would actually show up. There was no way for Gaston to know how persuasive he had been. But he would not be delayed longer. He would continue south whatever the size of the following. He knew he would meet at least some fellow Fairhopers in St. Louis and that others would join them in Mobile or in Baldwin County. Together, however many or few, they would have to do the job.

Democratic movements, Lawrence Goodwyn argues in his study of Populism, are launched by men and women with high levels of self-respect. They are neither "resigned" nor "intimidated," he writes. "They are not culturally organized to conform to established hierarchical forms. Their sense of autonomy permits them to dare to try to change things by seeking to influence others."[161] Gaston fitted this mold. Far from being intimidated by the status quo, he spent most of his thinking hours imagining how to create a society fundamentally different from the one into which he was born. He had the self-confidence to urge others to join him in taking large risks with their personal lives, just as he was doing with his own. There was also his deep need to be creative, to harness his restless energy and disciplined mind to some large venture. The Populist interlude, after the disappointing failure of the National Cooperative Company venture, had been satisfying and instructive, and had broadened him in many ways. But the political process never fully answered his needs. The challenge of creating a "model community" did. Mixing his bright optimism with the thrill of that challenge, he headed south.

When they left Des Moines, Gaston was a week away from his thirty-third birthday; in two weeks he and Clara would celebrate their seventh wedding anniversary in their new home; a month after that, on Christmas eve, she would be thirty-two years old. The youngest of their four children, all of whom were bundled up for the trip, was Leah Catherine, just a year old—walking, but still in diapers. Cornelius Alonzo, who would one day succeed his father as secretary of the colony, had just passed his third birthday; James Ernest was four; Frances Lily, five.

The last time Gaston had taken the Des Moines to St. Louis train, in early 1892, he had been with General Weaver on his way to cover for the *Tribune* the meeting of insurgents who would create the Populist Party. He met fellow reformers from the South there for the first time. In fact, the two largest delegations at that St. Louis meeting were from the

E.B. and Clara Gaston, on the eve of their departure for Fairhope, with their four children: Frances Lilly, Leah Catherine, James Ernest, and Cornelius Alonzo.

southern white and southern colored alliances.[162] Now, as he mused on the same train nearly three years later, he must have wondered how his group of northern reformers would be received in the deep South. He had no Populist connections in Baldwin County, and Norton, the helpful single taxer from Daphne, was himself a New Englander. He resolved to be prudent, sensitive to local custom, and tolerant of criticism.[163]

Early the next morning the train pulled into St. Louis's Union

Station, a magnificent structure that seemed to Gaston an auspicious setting for a rendezvous of colony builders. The sky was still overcast, but as they stepped from the train the travelers were cheered to see two strangers wearing "Fairhope" badges. These were Gilbert Anderson, a local twenty-nine-year-old Swedish-born carpenter, a member of the association for several months, and George Boeck, an older man, a Nebraska farmer. After a large breakfast at Anderson's nearby boarding house, Gaston set out to visit St. Louis single taxers, especially the Brokaws whom he regarded as among the association's most helpful supporters. In the late afternoon everyone returned to Union Station, put on "Fairhope" badges, and waited for the five o'clock train from Minneapolis, bringing additional colonists, the Dellgrens and the Tuvesons.[164]

An enthusiastic, optimistic member, August Dellgren was an avid recruiter as well. Born in Sweden, he was pastor of a Universalist church in Minneapolis and publisher of a Swedish-language religious and single-tax journal. At forty-six he was eager to start a new life based on what he called the Georgist spirit of justice and love for mankind, a passion apparently shared by his wife, Rachael, and he urged his parishioners to become Fairhopers with him. He had proudly written to Gaston that at least three families were ready to join the association. One of them, the Tuvesons, came with him to St. Louis.[165] Like the Dellgrens, Olaf and Anna Tuveson were Swedish-Americans. A painter, Olaf was thirty, four years younger than Anna. Their three children, all in tow, ranged in age from six months to four years.[166]

A St. Louis *Post Dispatch* reporter came by for an interview, and shortly before train time some of Anderson's friends came to see him off and to wish the Fairhopers well. The train left at 8:35 p.m. The strangers

**The route south, from Des Moines to Mobile,
on the Mobile & Ohio railroad.**

would have two nights and a day on board to get acquainted. It was not long, Gaston wrote, before they became "thoroughly at home with each other." There was plenty of time to exchange ideas, share visions of the cooperative commonwealth, and lay plans for the conduct of the colony. There must also have been personal details to share, and when the Gastons discovered they had left Leah's diapers in St. Louis, the Tuvesons came to their rescue.[167]

It was just before daybreak on the morning of the fifteenth when the long train journey ended in Mobile. There was a light breeze blowing out of the north, the air was crisp, and the promise was for a fair day. Jimmy Hunnell, mistaken about the arrival time, did not meet the train and did not catch up with the group until the early afternoon, but George Pollay and his wife, Jenny, had arrived the day before from Los Angeles, and were there to meet the travelers. Pollay was in his forties and originally from Vancouver, British Columbia. He was not entirely a stranger to the area because he had sailed the Gulf waters as a seaman two decades earlier. Letters to secretary Gaston from and about Pollay reveal a man who was an avid single taxer, drawn to the colony because of its emphasis on individualism and wary of what he called collectivism.[168]

Gaston seldom passed up an opportunity to discuss reform ideas but on this occasion he was captivated by the exotic sights and smells of the port city. With his fellow Fairhopers he wandered the wharves, inspected the markets, and gazed with fascination on the wild turkeys and deer shot by a hunting party just returned on the morning boat from Baldwin County. That sight persuaded him that "with a proper effort we need not lack for food in this country." The Fairhopers' "country" lay across Mobile Bay, on the eastern shore. To reach it they left on the

The *James A. Carney* took the Fairhopers on the last leg of their journey, from Mobile to Battles.

steamer *James A. Carney* at three in the afternoon, "eager for a glimpse of what seemed as the 'promised land.'" Everyone was moved by the excitement and the beauty of the crossing. The temperature had risen to the low sixties, but the day had become somewhat hazy so that

> the eastern shore did not come into view until we were well out in the bay, but then it loomed up so that we could hardly realize we were still several miles from it. To us who came, as some of us did, from far inland and had never seen salt water, the bay was . . . a source of keen delight. The water was rippled by a gentle breeze and wild ducks in countless numbers floated

106

"Sea Cliff," the highest coastal promontory between New Jersey and Mexico, two miles north of the Fairhope site.

on its surface, lazily taking wing as we drove toward them, and settling again on either side. Now and then one specially fat and heavy one, after beating the water in a vain effort to rise, would seek safety beneath the surface, while an occasional glimpse of the huge black fins of a porpoise above the water, or the glittering sides of a smaller fish leaping into the air in an effort to escape from its pursuers, testified to the wealth of food beneath the waves.

The *Carney* put in first at Howard's Wharf, at Daphne, where the group met Norton; Hunnell had arranged for them to stay in Battles Wharf, a village seven miles farther south, and so they exchanged hasty greetings and shoved off to continue their journey. Soon they were admiring the beauty of the eastern shore, "now rising in bold red cliffs to a height as at Montrose of nearly 100 feet, and again low where some little stream discharged its crystal waters in the bay." They tied up at Battles "just as night was settling down on bay and shore."[169]

Stepping onto the wharf at Battles, they were surprised to be greeted by Calvin B. Power, a member who was not expected this early. Older than the other Fairhopers—he was fifty-six and the father of two grown sons—Power was a Pennsylvania Populist who had just completed an unsuccessful campaign for Congress, a run he said he made to advertise the single tax. He and Mrs. Power, his third wife, had arrived on the fourteenth. Gaston would later describe them as an elderly couple for whom the rigors of pioneer life were too much, causing them to return early to their home in Dunbar, Pennsylvania. While they were in the colony, however, they were warm and sympathetic members, remembered for nursing the Gastons' baby, Leah, through her first Baldwin County illness.[170]

From the boat landing the settlers made their way to "Buck" Baldwin's nearby hotel where the women and children were left to spend the night. The men then followed a neighbor as he guided them through the woods with a pine torch to a log cabin that Jimmy Hunnell had secured for them. There they spread pallets on the floor and slept, or tried to sleep, and got to know the "festive Baldwin County fleas" who "disputed occupancy" with them and kept them "tossing and scratching till day-light."[171]

Before a nose count could be made the next day a covered wagon drove into "Camp Fairhope," ending a journey begun over a month earlier in Findlay, Ohio. These latest arrivals were Eleazer and Sylvania Smith and their two young children, George and Ethel. The Smith family saga—their celebrated departure from Ohio, vicissitudes along the way, and their determination to be the first on the grounds in Baldwin County—had been told in the *Courier*. They drove all night on the fourteenth to be there at roundup time, only to find that they had come to the wrong place. With outdated information, they had expected the meeting to be in Daphne and, in fact, had been on the wharf there the previous afternoon when the *Carney* docked. Disappointed, they drove through to Battles early the next morning. There was a special welcome for them when they arrived for they were among the most enthusiastic of members and much advance publicity celebrated their devotion to the cause. A forty-four-year-old baker, Eleazer Smith was described in one letter as a "hustler" not afraid "to tackle anything." Sylvania, forty-one, was "a good second." Another Findlay correspondent valued the Smiths as "two noble souls with hearts that will spread all over 'Fair Hope' Colony," and said of Sylvania that she fully supported the colony idea because she "wants a home where people will live for each other and heart respond to heart."[172]

Two young men, friends from Bayard, Iowa, completed the roster of the Fairhope vanguard. N. L. Mershon was Clara Gaston's nephew; J. T. Kearns was the husband of one of her nieces. The records do not tell us how Mershon and Kearns reached Battles, only that they were there. Neither was a member of the association, although Kearns would apply for membership the next summer.[173]

Altogether, then, "Camp Fairhope" was populated that first morning by twenty-eight persons. There were the Gastons, the elder Hunnells and their son, Jimmy, from Des Moines; young Mershon and Kearns from Bayard, Iowa; the Dellgrens and Tuvesons from Minneapolis; Gilbert Anderson from St. Louis and George Boeck from Nebraska; George and Jenny Pollay from Los Angeles and Vancouver; Calvin B. Power and his wife from Dunbar, Pennsylvania; and the Smith family from Findlay, Ohio—seven couples, nine children, five single men. Mostly strangers to each other, all strangers to their environment, they were drawn together by the vision of a better life in a community that would transform ideals and theories into nurturing realities. Now the time had come for them to create such a model community.[174]

Gaston brought with him from Des Moines an option to buy a parcel of bay-front land about two miles north of "Camp Fairhope." Eager to see where their model community might be built, the colonists made one of their first trips along the sandy, narrow road from Battles to the site. These first days were also taken up with finding a place to live, electing officers from among those on the ground, and getting acquainted with the county and the Eastern Shore.[175]

Baldwin County was the largest county in Alabama, one of the most spacious east of the Mississippi, seventy-two miles from north to south, and some thirty-two miles wide. Fewer than eleven thousand persons—about seven to a square mile—lived in this expanse. Plantation slavery along the rivers in the northern part of the county had flourished on cotton culture in the antebellum years. By the time the colonists arrived, however, staple-crop agriculture had disappeared. The Baldwin County economy they came to know was rooted in subsistence and truck farming, lumbering, and naval stores and was chiefly distinguished by stagnation.[176]

The county was too large and inaccessible for Fairhopers to think of it as home. Instead, their immediate world and frame of reference was the Eastern Shore, a seductive section of the county stretching for twenty miles or more along the coast from the river estuaries in the north to Weeks Bay in the South and running inland along the way from four to seven miles. The shore line was beautiful and peaceful. Sandy beaches reached back to tree-lined bluffs of heights varying from one or two feet to nearly a hundred feet at Montrose, the highest coastal prominence between New Jersey and Texas. Freshwater streams, a marvel to all who wrote about their first visits to the area, cut through the shore every so often, emptying clear, cold water into the Bay. The Bay itself could churn up ominously during a squall, but generally it was unmenacing. With no undertow, only slight tidal changes, and a gradually deepening shelf of firm, sand bottom, it was an almost perfect body of water for landlubbers such as the newly arrived Fairhopers. Fish were plentiful and easy to catch; swimming was safe and inviting; and the sunsets were a source of stunning beauty.

The natural inland boundary of the Eastern Shore was Fish River, a deep, fresh water river that meandered from Weeks Bay northward. Between the Bay and the river was table land thickly covered with pine trees. The whole area, 112 square miles, was sparsely settled. When the colonists arrived there were about 2,400 people living there—fewer than five families, on the average, per square mile. Fifty-five per cent of the people were white, mostly native born, mostly descended from antebellum independent farmers and poor whites. Among the blacks, whose proportion of the population had begun a long-term decline, were immigrants from other parts of the South—refugees from slave plantations—as well as a prominent group of mulattoes, most of whom

111

were descended from free people of color. Daphne, the county seat, Montrose, Battles, and Point Clear—all on the shore—were the principal population centers. Each of these places, but especially Point Clear, with a famous resort hotel, had long been a favored spot for summer homes for Mobilians. By 1894, however, many of these homes stood empty and, in truth, there were relatively few of them. The permanent residents eked out a modest living, a few of them from the Bay, many more from the poor soil that reluctantly supported subsistence and truck farming, and a goodly number who lived off the ubiquitous pine trees, cutting them for lumber or slashing them to drain the resin they yielded. A knowing and critical eye would not have looked upon the Eastern Shore as a promising site for a prosperous community and a skeptic might well have wondered about the prospects for a community based on land-value taxation built on land with so little value.

If such doubts troubled the pioneer Fairhopers they left no record of them. Gaston conceded that some of the other sites they had considered might have yielded a more abundant material life, but he was fond of repeating Bellangee's promise that "a living would be much more worth the making here."[177] Reassuring each other about their choice, the colonists busied themselves with the details of settling in. The Gastons and Hunnells remained in the log cabin where they had spent the first night, using it both as home and as headquarters for the association. The Dellgrens and Pollays rented a large home in Battles; the Smiths found a place nearby, and the Tuvesons settled farther to the north, close to the site that would be purchased in December.

Meanwhile, a special election was held on November 26. President Clements was the only non-resident continued in office. All of the other former officers who had declined to make the journey were put aside in favor of those who were on the grounds. From this time on, only those present at election time would choose officers and manage the colony affairs. This was the time, too, when the colony's theoretical commitment to equal rights for women was first put into practice, as women became association officers. E. B. and Clara Gaston along with August and Rachael Dellgren, Eleazer and Sylvania Smith, Calvin Power, George Pollay, and Jimmy Hunnell constituted the new governing group. The December 1 issue of the *Courier*, written in Battles and printed in Daphne, appeared a little late, but it carried fresh and encouraging news to distant members and friends.

By early December the Power family had returned to Pennsylvania. Anderson, holding to his original plan, had returned to St. Louis, expecting to return to Fairhope later. Boeck, accustomed to rich prairie land, found the Baldwin County soil and agricultural prospects poor; he left shortly after he arrived.[178] These departing Fairhopers were succeeded by a small group of newcomers. First to come was Maurice Michaels, a young carpenter from Minneapolis, another friend and recruit of Dellgren; he left his wife and two small children behind while he prepared for them to join him later. Michaels came on the twenty-fifth of November. Five days later, on the thirtieth, Clement L. Coleman arrived from St. Paul, Minnesota. Destined to be one of the key figures in the colony's early history, the Canadian-born Coleman (who apparently did not know Dellgren or any of the other Minnesota Fairhopers) was a forty-two-year-old machinist and aspiring orchard expert who leaned more to the cooperative than to the individualist side of the communitarian reform movement. He had come to Des Moines in September to visit Hunnell and Gaston, and they apparently made a strong impression on him. He left behind a wife and an eleven-year-old son who, as it turned out, never joined him.[179]

Three more recruits came to Camp Fairhope before Christmas. Amelia Lamon, a physician from Cincinnati, arrived about the first of the month. A widow with musical and literary talents, she was the first single woman in the colony; she was elected vice president in January. Peter Keil, a twenty-four-year-old Californian, feeling oppressed by hard times and unemployment, arrived early in the month. Finally, on Christmas eve, Andrew Larson from Minneapolis came. A friend of the Tuvesons, and a member of Dellgren's church, Larson was a thirty-nine-year-old Swedish-born shoemaker who found work to do almost immediately. He was joined in the next year by his wife and two children.[180] Larson came just in time for what Gaston described as a "grand 'co-operative' Christmas dinner" at the large home occupied by the Dellgrens and Pollays. The house was beautifully decorated with magnolia leaves and youpon, whose "brilliant red berries contrasted sharply with their green foliage." There were festoons of Spanish moss, an exotic novelty to all of them, and "many a branch of mistletoe." After the dinner, just as the sun began to set in the Bay, the entire contingent of Fairhopers, children as well as adults, walked the short distance to the Smith home "and spent the remainder of the evening making the walls of the old house resound with mirth and music."[181]

The January 1 issue of the *Courier* reported the happy Christmas celebration of Fairhopers, but the big news it carried to friends in the north was spread under the banner headline, "The Site Secured." Consisting of 132 acres of bay-front land midway between Montrose and Battles, this first purchase was hailed as "one of the most beautiful . . . and desirable spots for our purposes along the whole eastern shore of Mobile Bay." It ran about 2,800 feet along the bay front with a depth varying from 2,000 to 2,600 feet and was acquired at a cost of $771, or just under six dollars an acre.[182] Gaston was ecstatic about it but his description was surely written in part to entice a new wave of settlers:

> Here we have a short strip of sandy beach, then a narrow park ranging in width from 100 to 250 feet and covered with almost every variety of shrub and tree which flourishes in this locality—pine, live oak, magnolia, cedar, juniper, cypress, gum, holly, bay, beech, youpon and myrtle. On the east side of this "lower park," as we call it, a red clay bluff rises up almost perpendicularly to a height of nearly 40 feet. Along its serried edge tall, arrowly pines stand like sentinels looking out to sea. . . .
>
> From the top of the cliff, looking out above and between the lower rooted trees the bay spreads in all its beauty, with here and there a white sail or over in the channel toward the western shore, the smoke of a steamer or the bare poles of a ship. . . . On an ordinarily clear day the western shore may be plainly seen and in the background to the northwest the spires and smoky chimneys of Mobile.
>
> The ground gradually rises from the top of the cliff on an even and gentle slope (one of its chief beauties) for its entire depth, making the bay visible from almost any point. On the south portion, where our first settlement of Fairhopers will be made, about six hundred feet back from the top of the cliff, a beautiful knoll rises a few feet above the general slope.

Adjoining this land in the rear were two hundred additional acres for which a sale price of $250, or $1.25 an acre, had been agreed upon. The estate holding the land had additional acreage available at the same price; negotiations were proceeding. Those who had stayed away or withheld support should now reconsider. The colony was going to be a success. Already a road was being cut through the cliff down to the bay, the company store was under construction, and the first houses were ready to go up. Inquiries had reached the new association headquarters from many people who were "highly pleased with the . . . colony prospects." Fairhopers were feeling "greatly embarrassed by a lack of proper facilities for the entertainment of friends from the north who come to visit us or who write asking for accommodations."[183]

Now was the time for single taxers to come to Fairhope's aid. In the strongest plea he had ever made to them, Gaston stressed the accomplishments and pictured for them the possibilities. He wanted ten thousand dollars contributed to a "Single Tax Land Fund." That would make possible a colony nearly four miles square, a model single-tax community of ten thousand people. There were some single taxers who could give this entire amount, he wrote, with perhaps a trace of resentment at their previous stinginess toward his venture, "but it would take only one hundred men with $100 each, or one thousand men with $10 each. What an opportunity!" With unrestrained optimism he promised to publish "a goodly list of those who have responded to this appeal" in the next *Courier*.[184] Why should they not contribute? After a year of the most serious thought and careful planning Fairhope had now become a reality.

But what kind of reality?

The site was enchanting, but for his friends and likely benefactors and recruits in the north Gaston put a gloss on his description of it. He shaded no truth in writing of the natural beauty, but he passed silently over less compelling realities. Years later he admitted that "the whole tract was thickly covered with young pine timber" in which he often got lost on night visits to Jimmy Hunnell. Never previously able to sustain men and women in search of a living, the colony site had been called New City Hill, after an abandoned antebellum community named Alabama City which itself was built on the site of the earlier failed town of Clifton. Now it went by the name of Stapleton's Pasture because the beef cattle of a family named Stapleton roamed across it. It was, Gaston later said, "the wildest spot along the Eastern Shore from Battles to Daphne."

But it was more than wild. Isolated from the larger world by the bay and lacking commercial and financial institutions to turn to, the colonists would have to depend almost entirely on their ingenuity in fashioning their "model community" where they were with what they had. This, as they soon discovered, was not much. Judge Charles Hall, reminiscing later about his days as Baldwin County tax collector, recalled that Stapleton's Pasture was a huge thicket with few people and virtually no value. The few blacks in the area used to tell him, "but boss, this land aint worth nothing." Their plea to the tax collector was shaped by self-interest, but it was also good economic analysis. The Alyeas, with the authority of Paul Alyea's expertise as an economist and his long study of the economics of the Fairhope community, write that "the soil of the Fairhope hinterland was poor and the topography irregular. Economists would have no difficulty in agreeing that Fairhope land was marginal, if not sub-marginal, for agricultural purposes."[185]

A financial cushion would have helped to soften the harshness. Some critics have argued that Gaston should have postponed the move

E.B. Gaston built the first homes on the Fairhope site for his family and his mother-in-law. They were completed in January 1895.

until the colony treasury had been better supplied with membership fees and contributions from well wishers and until more single taxers had been enrolled.[186] But he had not wanted to wait any longer. Now he was faced with the consequences of that decision. He put it directly to *Courier* readers in a sobering financial report that summed up the colony's material history. In the twelve months since its organization the association had received a total of $2,255.59 of which $2,206.90 came from membership fees and penalties, $43.69 from *Courier* subscriptions, and $5.00 from donations. All expenses, including Gaston's forty dollar monthly salary, had been paid out of this small sum. There was $428.38 in cash and bills receivable, but $250.00 of that was owed on the second land purchase. With all the expenses of constructing their community lying before them, and with an abundance of much-needed cheap land about them to be purchased, they had $178.38 left at their disposal.[187]

For some of the members these challenges were too much. A report of January 22, 1895, on "members in good standing," that is, those who had kept up with their five dollar monthly payments, conspicuously omitted the Dellgrens, Smiths, and Tuvesons. That left the job of community building up to the eight local members in good standing: C. L. Coleman; Clara and Ernest Gaston; Jimmy Hunnell; Amelia Lamon; Maurice Michaels; and George and Jennie Pollay. And before long half of them would drop out.[188] The Alyeas indulged a taste for understatement when they entitled their chapter on these events "An Inauspicious Beginning."[189]

This was hardly the debut Gaston had desired or predicted. But he had known adversity and disappointments before. His confidence may have been shaken in these first weeks, but his powerful mix of ambition and idealism, and his remarkable ability to see through to possibilities invisible to others, sustained him. He celebrated the fact that land had been acquired and work begun. He never lost faith that his own steadfast determination in a cause he knew was right would soon lead others to join him. At the grand Christmas dinner, before his comrades had begun to fall away, he spoke of the mission on which they were now launched. Standing tall and erect, he read to them a letter from a Kansas friend who predicted that "the weekly record of your Colony experiment will form the best and most interesting economic text book of this century."[190] E. B. Gaston believed deeply in that prophecy. Nothing could foil or diminish his determination to see it fulfilled. Forty years later he was still working to make it a reality.

Notes

¹ T. S. Eliot, *Four Quartets* (New York: Harcourt Brace & Co., 1943), p. 39.

² Lewis Mumford, *The Story of Utopias* (New York: Boni and Liveright, 1922), p. 11.

³ E. B. Gaston, "True Cooperative Individualism: An Argument on the Plan of the Fairhope Industrial Association," *Liberty Bell*, April 28, 1894.

⁴ Paul M. Gaston, "Irony in Utopia: The Discovery of Nancy Lewis," *Virginia Quarterly Review*, LX (Summer 1984), 473-487; *Women of Fair Hope* (Athens: University of Georgia Press, 1984); *A Utopian Heritage: The Fairhope Single Tax Colony* (Birmingham: Alabama Humanities Foundation, n.d. [1986]); "Fairhope: A Gilded Age Utopian Experiment," in Valeria Gennaro Lerda (ed.), *Campagna nell'Et Dorata: gli Stati Uniti tra utopia e Riforma* (Rome: Bulzoni, 1986); "Two Views of Utopia," *Virginia Humanities Newsletter* XVI (Winter 1990), 1ff.

CHAPTER ONE

⁵ Fairhope Industrial Association (FIA) Constitution, Preamble and Article II.

⁶ Preamble, National People's Party Platform, 1892; Ray Marshall, "Undemocratic America," *Southern Changes,* XIV (Spring 1992), 8-9.

⁷ For an authoritative discussion of communitarian reform movements in the era when Fairhope was founded see Robert S. Fogarty, *All Things New: American Communes and Utopian Movements, 1860-1914* (Chicago: The University of Chicago Press, 1990). See also Robert S. Fogarty, *Dictionary of American Communal and Utopian History* (Westport, Ct.: Greenwood Press, 1980), and Timothy Miller, *American Communes, 1860-1960: A Bibliography* (New York: Garland Publishing, Inc., 1990). The Arden, Delaware, residential single-tax community, founded early in this century, was inspired by Fairhope but never became a fully-developed community; it continues to exist and to await its historian.

⁸ *Eastern Shore*, July 1908, quoted in Paul E. and Blanche R. Alyea, *Fairhope, 1894-1954: The Story of a Single Tax Colony* (University: University of Alabama Press, 1956), p. 135.

⁹ Alice Herring, "The Spirit of Fairhope," and S. H. Comings, "Reasons for Living in Fairhope," *Fairhope Courier*, April 1, 1904.

¹⁰ John and Evelyn Dewey, *Schools of Tomorrow* (New York: E. P. Dutton & Co., 1915), pp. 315-16. On Marietta Johnson's career see Paul M. Gaston, *Women of Fair Hope* (Athens: University of Georgia Press, 1984), chap. 3; Laura Elizabeth Smith, "A Woman and Her Idea: Marietta Johnson and the School of Organic Education" (B. A. Thesis, Harvard University, 1991); Phyllis Marie Lobdell, "The Marietta Johnson School of Organic Education: An Historical Study"

120

(Ph.D. Dissertation, Auburn University, 1984); and Rocco Eugene Zappone, "Progressive Education Reconsidered: The Intellectual Milieu of Marietta Johnson" (M.A. Thesis, University of Virginia, 1982).

[11] The school lingered with small enrollments and ever-diminishing significance in the community long after Johnson's death until it was reorganized on a new site, without a high school division. A recently-established museum is devoted to keeping alive Johnson's memory and educational philosophy.

[12] An unofficial census in 1908, at the time of municipalization, showed 569 persons in the Fairhope city limits. Figures for subsequent years are as follows: 1920, 853; 1930, 1,549; 1940, 1,845; 1950, 3,354; 1960, 4,858; 1970, 5,720; 1980, 7,286; 1990, 8,485.

[13] In the 1992 Presidential election, the moderate Democrat Bill Clinton won 22.5% of the Fairhope vote; George Bush won 61.3%, Ross Perot, 16.2%. *Eastern Shore Courier*, November 7, 1992.

[14] David and Holly Franke, *Safe Places East* (New York: Warner Paperback Library, 1973), pp. 42-69.

[15] Calvin Trillin, "U. S. Journal: Fairhope, Ala.," *The New Yorker*, June 11, 1979, p. 91.

CHAPTER TWO

[16] Minutes, Fairhope Industrial Association (FIA), January 4, 1894. Ernest B. Gaston (hereinafter EBG), "True Co-operative Individualism: An Argument on the Plan of the Fairhope Industrial Association," *Liberty Bell*, April 28, 1894. See Appendix One for the full text of this essay and a commentary on its composition.

[17] *Farmer's Tribune*, August 10, 1892, January 31, 1894. During the period covered by this book this paper changed its name from *Iowa Tribune* to *Iowa Farmer's Tribune* to *Farmer's Tribune*; it will be cited hereinafter as *Tribune*; *Fairhope Courier* (hereinafter cited as *Courier*), February 1, 1898.

[18] *Tribune*, December 7, 1892; *Courier*, February 1, 1898.

[19] Minutes, FIA, January 4, 1894.

[20] "Ernest B. Gaston," in *Portrait and Biographical Album of Polk County, Iowa* (Chicago: Lake City Publishing Co., 1890), pp. 596-97; "Gaston, Ernest B.," in *Who Was Who in America*, I (1897-1942), 443; "Gaston, Ernest Berry," in Marcus Whitman (ed.), *American Reformers* (New York: The H. W. Wilson Co., 1985), pp. 342-43; Donald E. Dawson, "Meet Your Relatives: Gaston Clan" [genealogy of the Gaston family], May 24, 1977, copy in author's possession; Ella Frances Gaston Crawford, "Application for Membership to the National Society of the Daughters of the American Revolution," n.d., copy in author's possession; *Courier*, September 15, 1900; Miscellaneous genealogical notes on the Gaston family supplied me by William Quantz, copies in author's

possession; Interview, C. A. Gaston, July 31, 1978; Warren C. Scoville, *The Persecution of Huguenots and French Economic Development, 1680-1720* (Los Angeles: University of California Press, 1960), pp. 28-30.

[21] Charles Blanchard, "History of the Church of Christ in Iowa: James E Gaston," *Christian Worker*, XLII (September 1928), 10-11; Dawson, "Gaston Clan"; *Courier*, October 20, 1932; Des Moines, Iowa, *City Directory*, 1866-1877.

[22] Blanchard, "Church of Christ in Iowa," 10-11.

[23] EBG, "Something New: Given before Alethean Society, April 2, 1887," copy in author's possession; *The Delphic*, I (January 1885), 49, II (June 1886), 141-43; Interview, C. A. Gaston.

[24] Curiously, Gaston later gave his graduation date as 1887, not 1886. This date appears in a biographical sketch published as early as 1890 as well as in some subsequent summaries of his life. On the other hand, the registrar's record at Drake University shows him graduating in 1886. Lisa Briedis (Drake University reference librarian) to Paul M. Gaston, September 22, 1978. He is referred to as a member of the class of '86 in *The Delphic*, V (March 1889), 102. The account of the 1886 graduation ceremonies in the student magazine lists him among those receiving the degree of Bachelor of Commerce and lavishes praise on his commencement oration, "The Reign of Time." *The Delphic*, II (June 1886), 141-43. The handwritten text for this address is in a well preserved notebook. It is headed: "*The Reign of Time*. Delivered at the Commencement Exercises of Drake University. Jun 17—1887," copy in author's possession. I have concluded that he graduated in 1886, but I have not been able to explain the puzzling evidentiary contradiction.

[25] *The Delphic*, I (February 1885), 62; I (March 1885), 83; I (April 1885), 97-99; I (June 1885), 130; II (December 1885), 43; III (October 1886), 29; III (November 1886), 32; III (June 1886), 257; and IV (March 1888), 101. In 1904 a Fairhope friend said of E. B. Gaston's voice: "Mr. Gaston's is a bass of real power, yet exceedingly sweet." *Courier*, January 1, 1904. Clara Leah Mershon was born December 24, 1862. Like her husband, she came from a family of French Huguenots who fled religious persecution to find a home in America. The flight of Henri Marchand and the history of his descendants are recounted in Oliver Francis Mershon, *My Folks: Story of the Forefathers of Francis Mershon, M.D.* (Rahway, N.J.: Quinn & Boden Company, Inc., 1946). See also Grace Lucille Olmstead Mershon, *Our Pioneers East and West of the Mississippi; Family Sketches—Mershon: Andrew Mershon and His Descendants* (Rahway, N. J.: The Association of the Descendants of Henry Mershon, Inc., 1955).

[26] *The Delphic*, II (February 1886), 77; III (December 1886), 432; and III (January 1887), 59.

[27] EBG to F. M. Welch, September 19, 1890. Frances Lily, the first of the five children of Ernest and Clara Gaston, was born on January 5, 1889; James Ernest was born on June 2, 1890.

[28] EBG to T. E. Fogarty, November 7, 1890.

CHAPTER THREE

[29] Dorothy Ross, "Socialism and American Liberalism: Academic Social Thought in the 1880's," *Perspectives in American History*, XI (1977-1978), 11, 16, 30-32; Ely is quoted in Ross; Daniel Aaron, *Men of Good Hope: A Story of American Progressives* (New York: Oxford University Press, 1951), p. 56; EBG to C. S. Leroy, September 9, 1890.

[30] Dorah Logan to EBG, March 31, 1890; *The Delphic* VI (October 1889), 10; P. A. Armstrong to EBG, July 14, 1890.

[31] *Des Moines Daily News*, July 19, 1890; *Des Moines Leader*, July 20, 1890; *Iowa State Register*, July 20, 1890.

[32] Arthur E. Morgan, *Edward Bellamy* (New York: Columbia University Press, 1944), pp. 247-253.

[33] John L. Thomas, *Alternative America: Henry George, Edward Bellamy, Henry Demarest Lloyd and the Adversary Tradition* (Cambridge: Harvard University Press, 1983), p. 263.

[34] Dorah Logan to EBG, March 31, 1890. Logan, who had attended Drake with Gaston, wrote of *Looking Backward:* "I hope his book will do much good in agitating the question and getting men to see the desirability of it. . . . I would enjoy an evening at the Hall hearing the class discussion of it."

[35] Edward Bellamy to EBG, April 17, 1890.

[36] Edward Bellamy, *Looking Backward, 2000-1887* (Boston: Houghton, Mifflin and Company, 1890; 1888), pp. 42, 52, 53, 268.

[37] Ibid, p. 56; *Tribune*, April 2, 1890. On Bellamy's life, thought, and influence see Thomas, *Alternative America*; Morgan, *Bellamy*; Sylvia E. Bowman, *The Year 2000: A Critical Biography of Edward Bellamy* (New York: Bookman Associates, 1958); Sylvia E. Bowman (ed.), *Edward Bellamy Abroad: An American Prophet's Influence* (New York: Twayne Publishers, 1962); Everett McNair, *Edward Bellamy and the Nationalist Movement* (Milwaukee: Fitzgerald, 1957); Arthur Lipow, *Authoritarian Socialism in America: Edward Bellamy and the Nationalist Movement* (Berkeley: University of California Press, 1982); and John Hope Franklin "Edward Bellamy and the Nationalist Movement," *New England Quarterly*, XI (December 1938), 739-772.

[38] Charles Albro Barker, *Henry George* (New York: Oxford University Press, 1955), p. 302. Anecdotes about the powerful effects of *Progress and Poverty* abound. Writing on the dust jacket of the Schalkenbach edition of *Progress and Poverty*, the historian Eric F. Goldman says that "an enormous number of . . . men and women who were to lead twentieth century America in a dozen fields of humane activity, wrote or told someone that their whole thinking had been redirected by reading *Progress and Poverty* in their formative years." A former University of Virginia law professor recalls that "*Progress and Poverty* was the first book I ever read that set me on fire. I was fourteen

when I read it, living in the Bronx, poor, with poverty all around me, and *Progress and Poverty* seemed the answer. I haven't read it since then; maybe that's what's wrong with me." Interview, Kenneth Redden, October 30, 1979.

39 Daniel T. Rodgers, *The Work Ethic in Industrial America, 1850-1920* (Chicago: University of Chicago Press, 1978), p. 215; Robert H. Bremer, *From the Depths: The Discovery of Poverty in the United States* (New York: New York University Press, 1956), p. 23; Eric F. Goldman, comment on dust jacket of Henry George, *Progress and Poverty* (New York: Robert Schalkenbach Foundation, 1960; 1879). On George's life, thought, and influence, in addition to the works cited above, see Henry George, Jr., *The Life of Henry George* (New York: Doubleday and McClure, 1900); Anna George DeMille, *Henry George, Citizen of the World* (Chapel Hill: University of North Carolina Press, 1950); Edward J. Rose, *Henry George* (New York: Twayne Publishers, 1968); Steven B. Cord, *Henry George: Dreamer or Realist?* (Philadelphia: University of Pennsylvania Press, 1965); Robert V. Adelson (ed.), *Critics of Henry George: A Centenary Appraisal of their Strictures on Progress and Poverty* (Rutherford, N. J.: Fairleigh Dickenson University Press, 1979); George R. Geiger, *The Philosophy of Henry George* (New York: Macmillan, 1933); Eric F. Goldman, *Rendezvous with Destiny: A History of Modern American Reform* (New York: Alfred A. Knopf, 1952); and Thomas, *Alternative America.*

40 *Tribune*, January 16, 1889.

41 George, *Progress and Poverty*, pp. 8-10, 528.

42 In the summer of 1889 George described Bellamy's *Looking Backward* as "a castle in the air, with clouds for its foundation." Nonetheless, as his biographer writes, "he saw much good in the Nationalist movement" and he believed that the Nationalist Clubs "were doing good work—asking the right questions and forcing discussion." Barker, *Henry George*, pp. 540-41.

43 George, *Progress and Poverty*, p. 328.

44 Henry George, Jr., *Henry George*, p. 496n. George, Jr., credits Thomas G. Shearman, a corporation lawyer, with suggesting the term single tax. Barker agrees: "Thomas Shearman was the man, rather than George himself, who transformed 'the single tax' from useful phrase into name and slogan . . . in January 1887." Barker, *Henry George*, p. 518.

45 Henry George, *Social Problems* (New York: Robert Schalkenbach Foundation, 1940; 1883), pp. 181, 188; George's biographer, Charles Barker, tells us that "though the emphasis on the socialization of industry is light in *Progress and Poverty*, the author had actually been consistent for sixteen years in asserting that natural industrial monopolies ought to be publicly owned and operated." Barker, *Henry George*, pp. 426-27; see, also, Sidney Fine, *Laissez Faire and the General Welfare State: A Study of Conflict in American Thought, 1865-1901* (Ann Arbor: University of Michigan Press, 1956), p. 293.

46 Laurence Gronlund, *The Cooperative Commonwealth: In Its Outlines: An Exposition of Modern*

Socialism (New York: C. Y. Dillingham), pp. 9-11, 259-278; Fine, *Laissez Faire*, pp. 331-32; Bellamy, quoted in Thomas, *Alternative America*, p. 269.

[47] Thomas, *Alternative America*, p. 269; Arthur E. Bestor, Jr., "The Evolution of the Socialist Vocabulary," *Journal of the History of Ideas*, IV (June 1948), 259.

[48] Dorothy Ross, "Socialism and American Liberalism," 13, 29-30.

[49] Rodgers, *The Work Ethic*, pp. 212-13; Morgan, *Bellamy*, pp. 291-92; Barker, *Henry George*, pp. 437-38. Ronald Yanosky, author of a forthcoming history of the single-tax movement during George's lifetime, perceptively observes that George was keenly aware of the eclectic nature of reform thought during the Gilded Age, but he "found it deplorable." He believed that he had worked out a comprehensive political economy from which one could deduce a coherent strategy. The single tax was the essential first step in that strategy. George thus believed that the melding of many social theories could only prevent clear analysis and constructive action. Ronald Yanosky to Paul M. Gaston, January 7, 1993.

[50] Alan Trachtenberg, *The Incorporation of America: Culture & Society in the Gilded Age* (New York: Hill and Wang, 1982), pp. 93-100; Thomas, *Alternative America*, pp. 183-84; Henry George, Jr., *Henry George*, pp. 405-06. See also Leon Fink, *Workingmen's Democracy: The Knights of Labor and American Politics* (Urbana: University of Illinois Press, 1983), and David Montgomery, *The Fall of the House of Labor: The Workplace, The State, and American Labor Activism, 1865-1925* (New York: Cambridge University Press, 1987).

[51] In this respect Gaston was typical of the group of utopians Robert Fogarty calls "political pragmatists"; they "wanted to show the world and their fellow radicals that cooperation could work and that there was a way to implement socialism in hard times." For them, "the cooperative commonwealth became an alternative to ballot-box democracy and ineffective unionism." Idealists, "eager to test their faith," they rejected "parlor socialism" to become builders of socialist communities. Robert S. Fogarty, *All Things New: American Communes and Utopian Movements, 1860-1914* (Chicago: The University of Chicago Press), p. 18.

CHAPTER FOUR

[52] John L. Thomas, *Alternative America: Henry George, Edward Bellamy, Henry Demarest Lloyd and the Adversary Tradition* (Cambridge: Harvard University Press, 1983), p. 274.

[53] Quoted in Arthur Bestor, *Backwoods Utopias: The Sectarian Origins and the Owenite Phase of Communitarian Socialism in America, 1663-1829*, 2nd enlarged edition (Philadelphia: University of Pennsylvania Press, 1970; 1950), p. 12.

[54] Robert V. Hine, *California's Utopian Colonies* (Berkeley: University of California Press, 1953), p. 4; Ralph Albertson, "A Survey of Mutualistic Communities in America," *Iowa Journal of History and Politics*, XXXIV (1936), 375-444; Charles Gide, *Communist and Co-operative Colonies* (New York: Thomas Y. Crowell Company, 1930); William Alfred Hinds, *American Communities*

and Co-operative Colonies, 2nd revision (Philadelphia: Porcupine Press, 1975; 1908); Alexander Kent, "Cooperative Communities in the United States," *Bulletin of the Department of Labor*, XXXV (July 1901), 563-646; Carl J. Guarneri, *The Utopian Alternative: Fourierism in Nineteenth-Century America* (Ithaca: Cornell University Press, 1991); Robert S Fogarty, *Dictionary of American Communal and Utopian History* (Westport, Ct.: Greenwood Press, 1980); and Robert S. Fogarty, *All Things New: American Communes and Utopian Movements, 1860-1914* (Chicago: The University of Chicago Press, 1990).

55 Albert Kimsey Owen, *Integral Cooperation: Its Practical Application* (New York: J. W. Lovell Co., 1885); Fogarty, *All Things New*, p. 122; EBG to Chas. W. Moore, October 3, 1890; EBG to A. K. Owen, May 31, 1891. The Topolobampo colony's history is told in Ray Reynolds, *Cat's Paw Utopia* (El Cajon, CA.: Privately Printed, 1972), and Thomas A. Robertson, *A Southwestern Utopia* (Los Angeles: Ward Ritchie Press, 1964). For a discussion of Marie Howland's relationship to the colony see Paul M. Gaston, *Women of Fair Hope* (Athens: University of Georgia Press, 1984), pp. 43-48, and Dolores Hayden, *The Grand Domestic Revolution: A History of Feminist Designs for American Homes, Neighborhoods, and Cities* (Cambridge, Ma.: MIT Press, 1981), pp. 103-13. Holly Blake is writing a much-needed biography of Howland.

56 J. J. Martin to EBG, June 2, 1890, and July 8, 1890; EBG to Chas. Evans Holt, January 12, 1891. The best history of Kaweah is in Hine, *California's Utopian Colonies*, pp. 78-100; a good short survey, with numerous photographs, is in Paul Kagan, *New World Utopias: A Photographic History of the Search for Community* (New York: Penguin Books, 1975), pp. 84-101.

57 Hine, *California's Utopian Colonies*, pp. 85-86. A Bellamy scholar notes that "Bellamy personally was consistently hostile to the idea of establishing socialist colonies, pointing out the need for a 'national' solution." Arthur Lipow, *Authoritarian Socialism in America: Edward Bellamy and the Nationalist Movement* (Berkeley: University of California Press, 1982), p. 88n; W. G. Niemeyer to EBG, July 10, 1890; G. W. Hansen to EBG, October 24, 1890; EBG to to G. W. Hansen, October 3, 1890; EBG to Chas. Evans Holt, December 22, 1890, and January 12, 1891.

58 *Tribune*, July 16, 1890; Des Moines *Daily News*, July 19, 1890; Des Moines *Leader*, July 20, 1890; *Iowa State Register*, July 20, 1890. A short article in the St. Louis *Globe Democrat*, July 20, 1890, was cited by several of those who wrote for particulars. This article, headlined "To Organize on the Bellamy Plan," was apparently reprinted in numerous small papers around the country.

59 Thom. G. H. Simson to Honorable Investigating Club, August 26, 1890 (translated by Christine Totten); Nicholas Brook to EBG, July 26, 1890; Fred D. Festner to Mrs. S. Gillette, August 15, 1890; Fred D. Festner to EBG, August 26, 1890, October 9, 1890.

60 EBG to Joshua Roberts, October 20, 1890.

61 Gaston took the journal containing copies of his letters to Fairhope in 1894; it suffered water damage in a 1906 hurricane and a few pages were victims of Gaston children drawings, but

most of it is legible.

[62] Ibid; EBG to R. T. Chase, November 5, 1890; EBG to John McLeod, October 13, 1890; EBG to Morris Woodward, n.d. [October 1890.]

[63] EBG mailed the last National Cooperative Company prospectus to A. K. Owen in 1891. He asked Owen to return it, but one does not exist in the archives. EBG to A. K. Owen, May 31, 1891. The best sources for the details of the colony plan are the accounts of it in the Des Moines newspapers. I have deposited in the FSTC archives a composite of the various newspaper accounts from July 1890 entitled "National Cooperative Company." To see how freely Gaston appropriated the language of the Kaweah constitution see Hine, *California's Utopian Colonies*, p. 87. See also Adam Behrman, "A Better Way: The Story of the National Cooperative Company" (Unpublished Seminar Paper, University of Virginia, 1984).

[64] "National Cooperative Company"; EBG to J. W. Edmiston, September 18, 1890.

[65] Rodgers, *The Work Ethic*, p. 214; "National Cooperative Company."

[66] EBG to H. Olerich, November 4, 1890; George, *Progress and Poverty*, p. 347.

[67] EBG to H. Olerich, November 4, 1890.

[68] It is not clear why Louisiana was the favored site. It appears, from numerous allusions in EBG's letters, that some of his group had personal connections with realtors there as well as personal interest in moving to the Lake Charles area where the colony was to be. His father-in-law already owned 160 acres of Louisiana land. EBG to T. E. Fogarty, October 13, 1890.

[69] The four original members, all of whom had made small contributions toward the $500 membership fee, were Gaston, E. D. Smith, J. P. Griffin, and Professor W. P. Macy. The only two persons who actually applied for membership and sent in a $5 down payment were Thomas Edward Fogarty of Moberly, Missouri, a forty-one-year-old boilermaker, and Ransford Talmage Chase, of Houston, Texas, a forty-two-year-old mechanical engineer. EBG to T. E. Fogarty, September 20, 1890; "Application for Membership in The National Co-operative Company." Fogarty's application is dated October 3, 1890, Chase's, October 17.

[70] EBG to R. W. Welsh, November 4, 1890; EBG to W. P. Macy, September 17, 1890; EBG to E. Dechamps, October 17, 1890; EBG to Wm. Cary, November 3, 1890; EBG to C. D. Otis, November 6, 1890; EBG to J. M. Frey, December 1, 1890.

[71] EBG to Fred Hancke, December 26, 1890; EBG to A. K. Owen, May 31, 1891.

[72] EBG to Nicholas Ward, November 18, 1890; EBG to Tom Smith, November 18, 1890; EBG to J. M. Frey, December 30, 1890; EBG to J. A. Pinkston, December 22, 1890, February 18, 1891; EBG to D. Appleton & Co., December 22, 1890; EBG to Wm. Wood & Co., December 26, 1890; EBG to F. R. Sanders, December 29, 1890.

CHAPTER FIVE

[73] *Tribune*, March 4, 1891; Gene Clanton, *Populism: The Humane Preference in America, 1890-1900* (Boston: Twayne Publishers, 1991), pp. 36-37.

[74] *Tribune*, March 18, 1891; Herman Clarence Nixon, "The Populist Movement in Iowa," *Iowa Journal of History and Politics*, XXIV (January 1926), 52-53.

[75] Lawrence Goodwyn believes that the Populist Party, which would come into formal existence within a year, was the creation of "the largest democratic mass movement in American history." It "challenged the corporate state and the creed of progress it put forward. It challenged, in sum, the world we live in today." Lawrence Goodwyn, *The Populist Moment: A Short History of the Agrarian Revolt in America* (New York: Oxford University Press, 1978), pp. vii, xxi.

[76] Edward Ayers says of southern farmers that they "thought public policy and private enterprise favored almost everyone in America other than themselves. Even though they produced more goods, paid more taxes, and cast more votes than any other group of Gilded Age Americans, farmers' voices often seemed to go unheard. Farmers felt abused by both of the major parties and exploited by every level of business from national corporations to local storekeepers." Edward L. Ayers, *The Promise of the New South: Life After Reconstruction* (New York: Oxford University Press, 1992), p. 214.

[77] Hamlin Garland, *Main-Travelled Roads* (New York: The Arena Publishing Company, 1891). "Under the Lion's Paw" was one of the most widely read and highly praised of the stories in the collection. Garland sometimes read it aloud at meetings of the insurgent farmers. The quotation is from the story "A Common Cause," first published in 1888. See Donald Pizer, *Hamlin Garland's Early Work and Career* (Berkeley: University of California Press, 1960), pp. 51, 95.

[78] Their formal names were the National Farmers' Alliance (The "Northern" or "Northwestern" Alliance); the National Farmers' Alliance & Industrial Union (The "Southern Alliance"); and the Colored Farmers' National Alliance and Cooperative Union (The "Colored Alliance").

[79] John D. Hicks, *The Populist Revolt: A History of the Farmers' Alliance and the People's Party* (Minneapolis: The University of Minnesota Press, 1931), p. 211.

[80] *Tribune*, May 6, 1891; May 20, 1891; Fred E. Haynes, *James Baird Weaver* (Iowa City: State Historical Society of Iowa, 1919), pp. 305-306.

[81] All twelve of his fellow Fairhope founders were associated with the *Tribune* or the Populist Party, or both, and it was during this period that he forged a close relationship with them.

[82] Harold U. Faulkner, *Politics, Reform and Expansion, 1890-1900* (New York: Harper & Row, 1959), pp. 130-131.

83 James B. Weaver, *A Call to Action: An Interpretation of the Great Uprising. Its Sources and Causes* (Des Moines: Iowa Printing Co., 1892), pp. 362, 378-380. Weaver probably began writing this very long book at the time Gaston joined the *Tribune* staff. It was published early in 1892. For Gaston's brief but flattering review see the *Tribune*, February 17, 1892.

84 *Courier*, February 16, 1912.

85 *Iowa State Register*, quoted in *Tribune*, June 3, 1891.

86 *Tribune*, May 13, May 27, and June 3, 1891.

87 Ibid., March 4, 1891. Judge W. F. Rightmire of Kansas installed the first local in Des Moines. Rightmire himself was not eligible to join the Farmers' Alliance, a fact that helps explain his key role in the Kansas Citizens' Alliance. Clanton, *Populism*, pp. 36-37.

88 *Tribune*, July 1, 1891; Bellamy's judgment is quoted in John L. Thomas, *Alternative America: Henry George, Edward Bellamy, Henry Demarest Lloyd and the Adversary Tradition* (Cambridge: Harvard University Press), p. 276; George's remarks, from his weekly newspaper, *The Standard*, are quoted in Charles A. Barker, *Henry George* (New York: Oxford University Press), p. 603.

89 Barker, *Henry George*, p. 604; Thomas, *Alternative America*, p. 310; Ronald Yanosky, "The Colored Farmers' Alliance and the Single Tax" (paper read at the annual meeting of the Organization of American Historians, 1992), cited with permission of the author.

90 Pizer, *Garland's Early Work*, pp. 48, 60, 62, 92-97; Jean Holloway, *Hamlin Garland: A Biography* (Austin: University of Texas Press, 1960), p. 67; Nixon, "Populist Movement in Iowa," 64.

91 The best short summary of the mature Populist demands is the 1892 National People's Party Platform, sometimes called the Omaha Platform. Works on the agrarian revolt and the Populist Party, often contentious and occasionally brilliant, abound. The most detailed narrative history, long the standard account, is Hicks, *The Populist Revolt*. Lawrence D. Goodwyn, *Democratic Promise: The Populist Moment in America* (New York: Oxford University Press, 1976), is likewise rich in detail and is a major reinterpretation; a scaled-down and more accessible version of Goodwyn's long book appeared two years later, with the title *The Populist Moment*. Clanton, *Populism*, is a useful up-to-date short overview with a good bibliographical essay.

92 Quoted in Goodwyn, *Populist Moment*, p. 95.

93 *Tribune*, August 19, September 30, 1891; Nixon "Populist Movement in Iowa," 57-58.

94 *Tribune*, February 24, 1892; Hicks, *Populist Revolt*, p. 227. With very little alteration, Donnelly's St. Louis speech became the preamble to the Omaha Platform.

95 *Tribune*, March 2, 1892; Hicks, *Populist Revolt*, pp. 169-70, prints the words of the song and

comments on the role of singing in the movement. Leonidas L. Polk of North Carolina would probably have been the nominee had he not died shortly before the convention. Many influential party leaders then preferred Walter Q. Gresham to Weaver, but they could not persuade him to accept the nomination. Hicks, *Populist Revolt*, pp. 232-235.

[96] Pizer, *Garland's Early Work*, p. 95.

[97] Quoted in Haynes, *Weaver*, p. 324; see also C. Vann Woodward, *Tom Watson: Agrarian Rebel* (New York: Rinehart & Co., Inc., 1938), pp. 234-235.

[98] H. Wayne Morgan, "Election of 1892," in Arthur M. Schlesinger, Jr., and Fred L. Israel (eds.), *History of American Presidential Elections, 1789-1968*, 4 vols. (New York: Chelsea House, 1971), II, 1784; Nixon, "Populist Movement in Iowa," 64.

[99] *Tribune*, March 30, August 10, 1892; July 26, August 16, September 6, September 13, November 15, November 29, 1893; January 24, 1894; Nixon, "Populist Movement in Iowa," 72; S. F. Davis to EBG, July 9, 1893; R. G. Scott and EBG to Dear Sir and Bro:, February 12, 1894; EBG, Untitled notebook [Financial Records of the Populist Party in Iowa], pp. 12-13.

[100] See, for example, E. A. Armstrong to EBG, April 10, 1894; J. Stemerdink to EBG, May 9, and August 30, 1894; J. O. Beebe to EBG, May 16, 1894; W. H. Russell to EBG, May 21, 1894; S. M. Gaston to EBG, June 24, 1894; Chas. C. Rodolf to EBG, July 3, 1894; Ed Lowrey to EBG, July 23, 1894; E. Healy to EBG, July 23, 1894; A. W. Ricker, to EBG, July 28, 1894; and *Tribune*, April 25, 1894.

CHAPTER SIX

[101] Gaston's correspondence for the period 1893-94 contains letters from ten persons with whom he had corresponded about the National Cooperative Company, all expressing interest in the new venture.

[102] EBG to Wm. Thaanum, August 20, 1893; T. Fulton Gantt to EBG, August 27, 1893; Hamlin Garland to EBG, November 18, 1893.

[103] Gaston may have passed the assignment on to Bellangee who had already read a paper before the World's Single Tax Conference at the Chicago World's Fair, entitled "The Relation of the Single Tax to Other Reforms." It was published under that title in the *Tribune*, December 27, 1893, and as "The Relation of the Land Question to Other Reforms," in *The Arena* IX (February 1894), 286-294; however, it did not mention other communitarian experiments, but focused on the unique appeal of the single tax as the essential first reform. On the other hand, the magazine's editor wrote to Gaston the following March urging him to get the article in by May 12. B. O. Flower to EBG, March 7, 1894.

[104] Lawrence Goodwyn, *The Populist Moment: A Short History of the Agrarian Revolt in America* (New York: Oxford University Press, 1978), p. xxiii.

[105] Charles Gide, *Communist and Co-operative Colonies* (New York: Thomas Y. Crowell Company, 1930), p. 11

[106] It is hard to prove a negative, but, with one exception, I have not found the term "cooperative individualism" in the literature of communitarian socialism, or anywhere else. In his recent history of American communes and utopian movements, Robert S. Fogarty mentions it only once—in reference to Gaston. Robert S. Fogarty, *All Things New: American Communes and Utopian Movement, 1860-1914* (Chicago: The University of Chicago Press), p. 169. It is also absent from Arthur Bestor's encyclopedic monograph, "The Evolution of the Socialist Vocabulary," *Journal of the History of Ideas*, IV (June 1948), 259-302. The one exception is an Iowan named Henry Olerich, one of Gaston's 1890 correspondents. In reply to Gaston's August 1893 inquiry, Olerich wrote: "I believe in 'Co-operative individualism' as outlined in 'A Cityless and Countryless World,'" a pamphlet Olerich had written. Henry Olerich to EBG, September 2, 1893. Later that year a very long utopian novel of the same title was published: Henry Olerich, *A Cityless and Countryless World: An Outline of Practical Cooperative Individualism* (Holstein, Iowa: Gilmore & Olerich, 1893). See also H. Roger Grant, "Henry Olerich and Utopia: The Iowa Years, 1870-1902," *Annals of Iowa* (Summer 1976), 349-361.

[107] Anna Bellangee Call, "Interesting Facts Given by Mrs. A. B. Call Re. Organization of Colony," *Courier*, April 28, 1949; J. Bellangee, "Fairhope, Its Problems and Its Future," *Single Tax Review*, XIII (May-June, 1913), 18; Paul E. and Blanche R Alyea, *Fairhope, 1894-1954: The Story of a Single Tax Colony* (University: University of Alabama Press, 1956), p. 12.

[108] "J. Bellangee," *Single Tax Courier*, April 20, 1895; Baldwin County, Alabama, Battles precinct, manuscript census, 1900; University of Illinois *Alumni Quarterly*, October 1913, in Bellangee Scrapbook (a collection of miscellaneous news clips).

[109] Herman Clarence Nixon, "The Populist Movement in Iowa," *Iowa Journal of History and Politics*, XXIV (January 1926), 30; Des Moines Single Tax Club Minutes Book; E. H. Gillette, "Eulogy to James Bellangee" (1915) in Bellangee Scrapbook; J. B. Weaver, Jr., to Anna Bellangee Call, September 16, 1915; *Courier*, September 1, 1894.

[110] Henry George, *Social Problems* (New York: Robert Schalkenbach Foundation, 1940; 1883), p. 191; Henry George, *Progress and Poverty* (New York: Robert Schalkenbach Foundation, 1960; 1879) pp. 456-57.

[111] The full text of the Cooperative Individualism essay, on which the following description and analysis is based, is reproduced in Appendix One.

[112] The constitution did include "transportation facilities" among the public utilities to be owned and run by the community. Well after the colony was established, Gaston formed a cooperative railway company which he called "The People's Railroad."

[113] Minutes, FIA, January 4, 1894. W. H. Sanders, one of those present at the January 4

meeting, wrote a letter from Fort Worth, Texas, on December 14, 1893, published in the *Tribune* on January 3, 1894, in which he said "I am anxious to see our colony completed and the location secured." One draws the inference from this that agreement on establishing a colony existed before the January 4 meeting. The "our" refers to Populists. Sanders was not a member of the Des Moines Single Tax Club. Fogarty's brief account of the origins of Fairhope states that "eleven members of the Des Moines Single Tax Club met in late November and early December 1893 to discuss the colony idea. Their December meeting was held in the home of General J. B. Weaver." Fogarty, *All Things New*, p. 170. The only source Fogarty cites here is the *Courier*, "August 1894." The August 15 issue of the *Courier*—the only "August 1894" issue—contains no mention of or allusion to the Des Moines Single Tax Club. The Club minutes report three meetings in 1893: November 23, December 7, and December 28. The December 7 meeting was at General Weaver's home with thirty-one persons in attendance; the previous meeting was attended by sixteen. According to the minutes the subjects of the three meetings were (1) November 23: "The Origins of Land Values"; (2) December 7: Thomas G. Shearman's view of the tariff; and (3) December 28: "The Political Economy of the Nazarine [sic]," a lecture by Weaver. It is certainly likely that the colony idea was at least discussed informally at one more of these meetings, but it was neither originated nor perfected in the Des Moines Single Tax Club; the club had only a peripheral relationship to Fairhope's gestation.

114 Gaston said on several occasions that the name Fairhope was the "happy thought" of Alf Wooster. See, for example, *Courier*, February 15, 1902, and September 21, 1933. In later years the credit was given, by others, to Clara Atkinson, Gaston's half sister. Anna Bellangee Call wrote in 1949 that "it has been the story, all the years I have been here, that the name Fairhope was the happy suggestion of Mr. Gaston's sister Dr. Clara Atkinson," one of the "legends" for which she said she had no "proof but word of mouth." *Courier*, April 28, 1949. C. A. Gaston, who succeeded his father as colony secretary in 1936, recalled many years later, when he was eighty-six, that Dr. Atkinson was always skeptical of her brother's idealistic plans; when she said perhaps he had a "fair hope" of succeeding he was inspired to choose the name Fairhope. Interview, C. A. Gaston, August 23, 1978. The Alyeas report both of these claims without deciding between them. Alyea and Alyea, *Fairhope*, p. 10n.

115 Bestor, "Socialist Vocabulary," esp. 283-284; Carl J. Guarneri, *The Utopian Alternative: Fourierism in Nineteenth-Century America* (Ithaca: Cornell University Press, 1991), pp. 93-120.

116 In 1904, when the ten-year Iowa charter expired, the Fairhope Industrial Association was incorporated under Alabama law and the name was changed to the Fairhope Single Tax Corporation.

117 *Tribune*, February 14, 1894; *The People's Tribune* (Saginaw, Michigan), July 6, 1894; Nixon, "Populist Movement in Iowa," 67. To sample the correspondence in which the link to Populism is made, see L. B. Baker to EBG, March 7, 1894; J. H. Hackman to EBG, February 19,

27, and March 5, 1894; J. H. Upton to EBG, March 3, 1894; Scott Wright to Alf Wooster, March 12, 1894; Eleazer Smith to EBG, June 20, 1894; C. B. Power to EBG, June 29, 1894; and J. N. Dixon to EBG, August 26, 1894.

[118] The officers chosen on January 31 were: L. R. Clements, President; Edward A. Ott, Vice-President; E. B. Gaston, Secretary; Alfred Q. Wooster, Treasurer and Superintendent of Finance and Insurance; James Bellangee, Superintendent of Land and Highways; T. E. Mann, Superintendent of Public Services; George B. Lang, Superintendent of Merchandising; James P. Hunnell, Superintendent of Industries; Andrew Engle, Superintendent of Public Health; and S. S. Mann, W. H. Sanders, and H. C. Bishop, Trustees.

[119] *Tribune*, June 8, September 7, 21, 1892, September 13, 1983.

[120] *Tribune*, April 22, 1891, November 29, 1893; Nixon, "Populist Movement in Iowa," 29, 31, 66-67; Sovereign was said to be "radical and controversial in his attitude" by Fred E. Haynes, *Third Party Movements Since the Civil War, with Special Reference to Iowa: A Study in Politics* (Iowa City: State Historical Society of Iowa, 1916), p. 334.

[121] *Tribune*, November 15, 1893, August 8, 1894.

[122] *Tribune*, April 22, 1891; January 27, 1892; July 8, 1891; January 27, October 26, 1892; August 19, 1891.

[123] The constitution is reproduced in Appendix Two.

[124] *Liberty Bell*, March 31, 1894. The quotation appeared on the masthead of the *Courier* from the first issue, August 15, 1894, until October 15, 1899.

CHAPTER SEVEN

[125] W. E. Brokaw to EBG, January 23, 1894. Gaston wrote in the *Courier* of October 1, 1894, that "our attention was first directed to this county by Editor Brokaw." In his many subsequent accounts of Fairhope's founding, he similarly credited Brokaw with directing him to Norton and Baldwin County. Brokaw had previously met Norton at a national single-tax conference. See *Courier*, February 1, 1898, and EBG, "Fairhope Single Tax Colony," in L. J. Newcomb Comings and Martha M. Albers, *A Brief History of Baldwin County* (Fairhope: Baldwin County Historical Society, 1928), p. 72.

[126] W. S. Morgan (secretary-treasurer of the National Reform Press Association) to EBG, May 4, 1894; Lawrence Goodwyn, *The Populist Moment: A Short History of the Agrarian Revolt in America* (New York: Oxford University Press, 1992), pp. 116-117, 206-212; *Tribune*, December 31, 1890; Minutes, FIA, May 18, 1894; L. H. Crampton to EBG, July 12, 1894; *Liberty Bell*, March 31, April 18, 1894; Alf Wooster to EBG, April 17, May 22, June 3, 1894. Originally published in Des Moines, the *Bell* was moved to Oskaloosa in the spring of 1894.

127 *Liberty Bell*, April 28, 1894. The $5 per month and $175 membership fee provision had been adopted by the executive council at its February 26 meeting: Minutes, FIA, February 26, May 11, 1894.

128 According to Fogarty's extensive list of communitarian experiments started between 1880-93, inclusive, only 6.7% were in the South; 36.7% were in the Plains and Rocky Mountain states; 30.0% were on the Pacific coast. This trend changed dramatically starting in 1894 when the Fairhopers moved south: half of the thirty-four colonies started between 1894-1899, inclusive, were in the South. Robert S. Fogarty, *All Things New: American Communes and Utopian Movements, 1860-1914* (Chicago: The University of Chicago Press, 1990) Appendix, pp. 227-233. See also, Otohiko Okugawa, "Annotated List of Communal and Utopian Societies, 1787-1919," in Robert S. Fogarty, *Dictionary of American Communal and Utopian History* (Westport, Ct.: Greenwood Press, 1980), pp. 209-226. Timothy Miller, *American Communes, 1860-1960: A Bibliography* (New York: Garland Publishing, Inc., 1990), is an invaluable guide to the study of these and other colonies.

129 *Tribune*, August 17, 1892.

130 Douglass is quoted in Fogarty, *All Things New*, p. 14.

131 On the Ruskin colony see John Egerton, *Visions of Utopia: Nashoba, Rugby, Ruskin, and the "New Communities" in Tennessee's Past* (Knoxville: University of Tennessee Press, 1977), chap. 4; Francelia Butler, "The Ruskin Commonwealth: A Unique Experiment in Marxian Socialism," *Tennessee Historical Quarterly*, XXIII (December 1964), 333-342; Fogarty, *All Things New*, pp. 154-161; and Miller, *American Communes*, pp. 446-453.

132 So far as I know, there is no study of the racial beliefs and practices of communitarian reformers in the emancipation and New South eras, but see R. Laurence Moore, "Flawed Fraternity—American Socialist Response to the Negro, 1901-1912," *The Historian*, XXXII (November 1969), 1-18; Sally M. Miller, "The Socialist Party and the Negro, 1901-1920," *Journal of Negro History*, LVI (July 1971), 220-229; James M. McPherson, *The Abolitionist Legacy: From Reconstruction to the NAACP* (Princeton: Princeton University Press, 1975); and David R. Roediger, *The Wages of Whiteness: Race and the Making of the American Working Class* (New York: Verso, 1991).

133 The classic account of southern Populism, stressing its impulse to forge alliances across the racial divide, is in three books by C. Vann Woodward: *Tom Watson: Agrarian Rebel* (New York: Rinehart & Co., Inc., 1938); *Origins of the New South, 1877-1913* (Baton Rouge: Louisiana State University Press, 1951); and *The Strange Career of Jim Crow*, 3rd. revd. ed. (New York: Oxford University Press, 1974).

134 *Tribune*, August 17, 1892.

135 Ronald Yanosky, "The Colored Farmers' Alliance and the Single Tax" (paper read at the annual meeting of the Organization of American Historians, 1992), quoted with permission of the author; the letter from Henry George to James E. Mills, October 12, 1890, is quoted by Yanosky.

[136] Henry George, *Progress and Poverty* (New York: Robert Schalkenbach Foundation, 1960; 1879), pp. 354-355.

[137] For a discussion of how the Fairhopers dealt with race in the first thirty years or so of the colony's history, see Paul M. Gaston, *Women of Fair Hope* (Athens: University of Georgia Press, 1984), pp. 1-18. Bellangee's report, summarized below, was published in *Liberty Bell*. The quotations here are from an undated news clip in the Bellangee Scrapbook.

[138] EBG to Rich M. Lucas, September 30, 1890.

[139] S. A. Hackworth to EBG, August 18, 29, 1890, December 29, 1893; EBG to S. A. Hackworth, August 26, September 15, 1890.

[140] They were sometimes evasive about specifying exactly what principles their colony would demonstrate. As one of them put it, "I think it is a mistake to put the question of single tax before every thing else. I have been cautious to keep it out of our conversations as I found it prejudiced our interests." S. S. Mann to EBG, July 15, 1894.

[141] J. Bellangee to EBG, June 4, 10, 14, 17, 20, July 3, 1894; *Liberty Bell* clippings, Bellangee Scrapbook; *Courier*, August 15, 1894.

[142] J. Bellangee to EBG, July 16, 1894.

[143] Paul E. and Blanche R. Alyea, *Fairhope, 1894-1954: The Story of a Single Tax Colony* (University: University of Alabama Press), p. 25.

[144] Minutes, FIA, August 10, 1894.

[145] Minutes, FIA, February 16, August 10, 1894.

[146] L. B. Baker to EBG, February 3, 1894; O. N. Bancroft to EBG, January 30, February 15, 1894; William A. Graves to EBG, March 31, 1894; Luke Rawlings to EBG, May 12, 1894; George Pollay to EBG, May 30, 1894; Gilbert Anderson to EBG, June 14, 1894; E. A. Phipson to EBG, April 24, 1894. Gaston received many letters from Topolobampo veterans, all burned by their experience there and anxious for more individualism.

[147] J. Bellangee to EBG, July 16, 1894.

[148] Minutes, FIA, February 6, 1894.

[149] L. B. Baker to EBG, August 3, 1894; *The Standard*, November 2, 1889, pp. 2-3; Fiske Warren, "Historical—United States," in Joseph Dana Miller (ed.) *Single Tax Year Book* (New York: Single Tax Review Publishing Co., 1917), pp. 66-67; I have found no independent evidence to support Warren's statement that George made a specific comment on Fairhope and I report it here with some skepticism. See also Geiger, *Philosophy of Henry George*, p. 444, and Arthur N. Young, *The Single Tax Movement in the United States* (Princeton: Princeton University Press, 1916), p. 256.

[150] *Courier*, December 1, 1898; George White to EBG, November 9, 1894; Bolton Hall to EBG, February 26, 1894; Jas. S. Reynolds to EBG, June 15, 1894.

[151] Jerry Simpson to EBG, February 27, 1894; Percy Pepoon to Alf Wooster, March 17, 1894; Clarence S. Moore to EBG, August 15, 1894. Garland's letter, obviously written as a promotional blurb, appeared originally in the *Single Tax Courier*; it was published in the *Courier;* October 1, 1894.

[152] Hamlin Garland to EBG, June 25, July 6, 1894; the quotation is from the second letter.

[153] I am indebted to Ronald Yanosky for helping me to reach this generalization about the national single-tax movement.

[154] Fogarty, *All Things New*, p. 156; Egerton, *Visions of Utopia*, pp. 68-86. Ruskin was at its zenith in 1897, with 1,800 acres of land, a diversified economy, a thriving school, and 250 residents from 32 states and 6 foreign countries. By the end of the century it had fallen apart. A dozen of its members moved to Fairhope.

[155] *Courier*, August 15, 1894.

[156] Ibid., September 1, 1894.

[157] The "roll of honor" actually included twenty-two names, but one of those members had recently died. *Courier*, August 15, September 1, 1894.

[158] Ibid., October 1, 15, 1894.

CHAPTER EIGHT

[159] Minutes, FIA, October 26, 1894. At this meeting Gaston and Hunnell were authorized to represent the association and, with three others selected by them from the members on colony grounds, to purchase land and conduct other business for the colony. *Tribune*, September 5, 1894; *Courier*, September 15, 1894; H. J. Woodhouse to EBG, September 6, 1894. The account of the journey from Des Moines to Baldwin County that follows is based in part on Gaston's contemporary history of the trip, a vivid piece published in the *Courier*, December 1, 1894. That account, however, has a typographical error, giving the month of departure as October instead of November, and the day of the month as the 13th instead of the 12th; it also misstates the time of the journey from St. Louis to Mobile to be twenty hours instead of thirty-three or thirty-four. According to the time tables I have located, Gaston left Des Moines at 6 p.m. on the evening of the 12th and arrived in St. Louis at 9:20 the next morning. The enlarged party left St. Louis at 8:35 p.m. on the evening of the 13th and arrived in Mobile at 6:00 a.m. on the 15th. For additional accounts of the journey, see *Courier* February 1, 1897; February 1, 1898; June 1, 1901; November 17, 1905; and December 4, 1908; St. Louis *Post Dispatch*, November 14, 1894; Mobile *Daily Register*, November 15, 16, 1894; EBG, "Fairhope Single Tax Colony," in L. J. Newcomb Comings and Martha M. Albers, *A Brief History of Baldwin County* (Fairhope: Baldwin County

Historical Society), pp. 3-4; Paul E. and Blanche R Alyea, *Fairhope, 1894-1954: The Story of a Single Tax Colony* (University: University of Alabama Press, 1956), pp. 27-30; Elof Tuveson, "Recollections," p. 1; and C. A. Gaston, various interviews.

[160] *Courier*, October 1, 15, 1894.

[161] Lawrence Goodwyn, *The Populist Moment: A Short History of the Agrarian Revolt in America* (New York: Oxford University Press, 1978) p. xix.

[162] C. Vann Woodward, *Origins of the New South, 1877-1913* (Baton Rouge: Louisiana State University Press, 1951), p. 242.

[163] Interview, C. A. Gaston, June 8, 1977.

[164] Gilbert Anderson Application for Membership, Fairhope Industrial Association, June 27, 1894; *Courier*, October 15, 1894; C. A. Gaston to Mrs. Gilbert Anderson, August 8, 1953.

[165] *Courier*, October 1, 1894; October 15, 1894; November 1, 1894.

[166] Ibid., November 1, 1894; Baldwin County, Alabama, Battles precinct, Manuscript Census, 1900.

[167] St. Louis *Post Dispatch*, November 14, 1894; *Courier*, December 1, 1894; Interview, C. A. Gaston, June 8, 1977, August 12, 1978. Gaston family anecdotes include the story of how Gaston returned to Anderson's boarding house to retrieve his typewriter, but forgot the diapers.

[168] George Pollay to EBG, June 15, 1894, August 18, 1894, September 5, 1894; James S. Reynolds to Clarence S. Moore, May 1, 1894; *Courier*, September 15, 1894.

[169] *Courier*, December 1, 1894.

[170] Ibid., December 4, 1908.

[171] Ibid., December 1, 1894, June 1, 1901.

[172] Ibid., October 15, December 1, 1894, December 4, 1908; J. D. Lucier to EBG, September 30, 1894; L. B. Baker to EBG, April 26, 1894; E. Smith to EBG, July 30, August 8, September 3, 1894.

[173] *Courier*, July 1, 1895.

[174] The list of colonists passing through St. Louis given in the November 14 *Post Dispatch* includes "Mrs. Dr. Lamon, Cincinnati." There is no mention anywhere of Amelia Lamon arriving with the first settlers. The *Courier* reports that she arrived about December 1. It seems likely that she met the group in St. Louis, determined then that she would become a Fairhoper, and then went on to Rome, Georgia, where her furniture was in storage. Amelia Lamon to EBG, October 12, 1894.

[175] An option for Gaston to buy 220 acres of land on Mobile Bay from Sarah I. Tatum, for

$6.00 an acre, was executed by Mrs. Tatum on August 14, 1894. When the association failed to send the required down payment, Mrs. Tatum notified Gaston that the option had expired but then promised to keep the land available for purchase by the Fairhopers at the same price until December 1. Sarah I. Tatum to EBG, October 17, 1894. The colonists signed a deed for the purchase of 132 of these acres on January 5, 1895; the rest was bought piecemeal, and at higher prices, over the next year. See Phil Townsend, "Land Acquisition and the Fairhope Single Tax Colony" (Unpublished Seminar Paper, University of Virginia, 1988), pp. 4-6.

176 Kay Nuzum, *A History of Baldwin County* (Bay Minette: The Baldwin Times, 1970), pp. 56, 87. Population figures are from the *Twelfth Census of the United States, 1900.*

177 *Courier*, February 1, 1898.

178 Ibid., May 15, 1904, December 4, 1908;

179 Ibid., October 1, December 1, 1894; Clement L. Coleman, Application for Membership, October 25, 1894; Baldwin County, Alabama, Battles Precinct, Manuscript Census, 1900.

180 Peter Keil to EBG, June 6, July 17, 1894; Clarence Moore to EBG, August 1894; *Courier*, January 1, 1895; December 1, 1898, October 1, 1901; Baldwin County, Alabama, Battles Precinct, Manuscript Census, 1900. Coleman remarried in Fairhope. He named his son Henry George Coleman.

181 *Courier*, January 1, 1895.

182 Tatum Deed, January 5, 1895; *Courier*, January 1 and February 1, 1895; Townsend, "Land Acquisition," pp. 4-5.

183 Ibid. Minutes, FIA, December 15, 17, 1894.

184 *Courier*, January 1, 1895.

185 EBG, *Quarter Centennial History: Fairhope Single Tax Colony, 1895-1920, With Added Material Bringing Story to August 1932* (Fairhope: Fairhope Courier Print Shop, 1932), pp. 4-5; Marie Bankhead Owen, *The Story of Alabama: A History of the State,* 5 vols. (New York: Lewis Historical Publishing Company, 1949), I, 363; *Courier*, February 1, 1898; Charles Hall, "Address," in *Twenty-Sixth Anniversary: Fairhope Single Tax Colony. Addresses, Messages, History, Songs* (Fairhope: Fairhope Courier Print, 1921), pp. 9-10; Alyea and Alyea, *Fairhope*, pp. 32-33.

186 Alyea and Alyea, *Fairhope*, p. 35.

187 *Courier*, February 1, 1895.

188 Minutes, FIA, January 22, 1895.

189 Alyea and Alyea, *Fairhope*, p. 27.

190 W. A. Wotherspoon to EBG, December 19, 1894; *Courier*, January 1, 1895.

Appendix One

TRUE COOPERATIVE INDIVIDUALISM

An Argument on the Plan of Fairhope Industrial Association[191]

The present social and economic order is doomed. In the height of its marvelous achievements it bears within itself the seeds of its own destruction. Clear headed economists and warm hearted philanthropists long ago pointed out and denounced its enormous waste of human energy and natural resources and its hideous injustice and cruelty. It has been "weighed in the balance and found wanting." It must go! that is settled! but the very serious fear presents itself that we who now recognize and denounce its evils and are striving to unite a majority of its victims for its overthrow, may go before it goes—in waiting the slow movement of

---

[191] Available evidence suggests that Gaston completed the first version of this essay in August of 1893 and that he sent it out then to a small group of men, most of whom he had corresponded with earlier about the National Cooperative Company, hoping to interest them in a new colony venture based on the ideas discussed in the essay. He probably revised it slightly when he read it to twelve Populist Party associates in his office on January 4, 1894. It was at this meeting that a decision was made to draw up by-laws and a constitution for a new community, based on the ideas presented in the essay. After the constitution was drawn up for the Fairhope Industrial Association the essay was put in its final form. It is this version that appears here. It was first published in *Liberty Bell*, April 28, 1894. It appeared in the *Courier*, shortly after the colony was established, in two installments, on February 15 and March 1, 1895. It was distributed, in printed forms that have not survived, well before this. One correspondent, for example, wrote to Gaston of having read his article on "Cooperative Individualism" three months before it appeared in *Liberty Bell*. D. N. Hartley to EBG, January 30, 1894.

majorities.

To the one who has the true spirit of a reformer present conditions are almost unbearable. Even though his own financial and social standing may be secure; the injustice and attendant want, misery, hardships and despair everywhere apparent fill his life with sadness—but the qualities of mind and heart which mark the reformer and philanthropist are a serious disqualification for financial success under existing conditions.

With the constant narrowing of opportunities, as one industry after another goes into the hands of trusts and the broad acres of our common heritage pass under the control of speculators, competition becomes so fierce that none can hope to succeed but those in whom heredity and training have most developed the commercial instinct.

The man who pauses in the mad rush for wealth to study the causes of increasing poverty amid rapidly accumulating wealth, or who knowing the cause, gives of his time and means to the enlightenment of his fellowmen is almost certain to fall far behind in the race and to be looked upon as a failure, not alone by those who have left him in the rear, but even by the more unfortunate for whom he has striven. Under the pressure of such circumstances the reformer must face the alternative of being true to his higher convictions at the expense of material comfort for the present and safe provision for the future, or, turning his back on what he knows to be his true self and higher convictions, pursue with the utmost concentration of his energies the prize of material gain.

There is but one way to escape this dire alternative—that the way pointed out, not alone by the natural promptings of the reformer's heart but, by the "logic of events" which has forced the fiercest antagonists in business into associations for mutual protection.

The earth is as fruitful, nature smiles as brightly, and rewards effort as bountifully as if no "inhumanity of man to man made countless thousands mourn."

What more reasonable, more practical, than for those who understand the devices by which the labor of the many is taken for the profit of the few, to unite for the elimination of the land speculators, the usurers, the monopolists of public service, and all the other parasites who fatten upon industry compelling the producer to gnaw the bone while they eat the meat.

Believing not only in the wisdom and practicability of such an effort, but that it offers the only hope of present escape from the deplorable conditions everywhere prevalent, the plans herein presented have been formulated for a model community to be free from all forms of private monopoly, and which will insure to its members equality of opportunity, the full reward of individual efforts and the benefits of co-operation in matters of general concern.

In presenting to our co-laborers in the work of economic reform these plans, we do so believing that they must appear to them as to us, an open door to wider opportunities for usefulness and greater possibilities of individual profit and enjoyment. Greater opportunities for usefulness, for they that shall make good theories work and prove the value of proposed social solutions by practical demonstration, will do far more to move the world than the wisest and most brilliant theorists. Greater possibilities for legitimate individual profit, because securing the full product of their labor and the opportunity to exchange it for the products of others with the minimum of friction and loss; and of happiness, because associated with congenial spirits and co-operating with them to secure the utmost of comfort and culture.

These plans are submitted not as the views of a dreamer but as a practical business proposition to practical men and women; not as plans requiring for their successful fulfillment, qualities properly supposed to belong to angels, (certainly not visible at present in human kind) but the result of the joint efforts of many, agreed on fundamental economic principles, to apply them in harmony with the known and constant springs of human action.

We have not been carried away by dreams of an ideal society from which selfishness was banished and men sought only the happiness and good of others.

We have sought to build for humanity as it is—not the worst, not the best—but plain every day average humanity seeking its own interest.

Our motto is not "each for all and all for each" but "every one for himself—under the law of equal freedom." Not "from each according to his ability and to each according to his needs," but "equal opportunities to all and to the laborer the full product of his labor."

The framers of the constitution of Fairhope Industrial Association have kept steadily in view two great laws of human nature and human rights: "All men seek to satisfy their desires with the least exertion" and "Every man has freedom to do all that he wills, provided he infringes not the equal freedom of any other man."

To the lack of a proper recognition of these fundamental principles may be traced the multitude of failures of social experiments which have done so much to discourage reformers and to strengthen the position of those who insist that what is, is right and must continue.

Ignoring the first, experiments in community building have utterly failed to measure the dominant forces of human nature. Failing to recognize the second, they have substituted the tyranny of the community for the tyranny of individuals, and the last state has been almost, if not quite, as bad as the first.

We believe that one of the most common and most grievous errors cherished by social reformers is that "Society" (with a big S) is possessed of rights and powers superior to those of its individual components. While vehemently denying the right of one individual to control of the person or products of another, they as vehemently assert the right of "Society" to direct the action of all individuals and determine the share of each in the joint product.

We hold that individuals have certain natural, inherent and inalienable rights which society cannot possibly acquire any right to suspend or abrogate and that chief among these is the right of each to the exercise of his own powers for his own benefit and to the use and enjoyment, equally with all others, of natural opportunities.

A Pure Democracy

In form and practice our community is to be a pure democracy. Every adult member, without regard to sex, having an equal voice in its affairs, PERSONS will rule instead of PROPERTY. The organization in this respect conforms more nearly to the rule in municipal corporations than to the ordinary corporations for pecuniary profit. There can under such rules be no possibility of a few stockholders, through the control of a majority of the stock, "freezing out" the remaining stockholders, sacrificing their interests of subverting their rights. Each member has for guarantee of the permanent enjoyment of the advantages obtainable through such organization, the like and equal interest of all his fellow members.

The Initiative And Referendum

By the initiative and referendum all legislative power is reserved in the whole people, and never delegated to a part, the powers and duties of the officers of the company being confined to executing the laws made by the whole membership and suggesting legislation to be submitted for their final approval or rejection. Partisan politics as now known, cannot exist with the initiative and referendum. Party tyranny which is almost always exercised in the interest of a few men is shorn of its power when measures are voted for instead of men.

142

Salaries Not To Exceed Average Earnings

By constitutional guarantee that salaries of officers shall not exceed the average earnings of like energy and ability in productive industry, the tendency to corruption in office and the creation of an office holding aristocracy, which is a marked feature of existing conditions, will be corrected. "Public office" will then indeed by a "public trust" and will be sought and bestowed as a recognition of ability and trust reposed, rather than for its opportunities of personal aggrandizement.

Land

In its provision for land holding and use, our plan applies in the only practical and satisfactory way the law of equal freedom, permanently securing the equal rights of all its members in the use of natural resources.

Obviously equal rights in land cannot be secured by an apportionment of equal areas because tracts of equal area vary greatly in value from differing advantages of location and natural qualities. Experience demonstrates, too, that even though an apportionment of equal values should be made, such values could hardly be expected to remain in equilibrium for a year, certainly not permanently. The only way to maintain this equilibrium, to secure from year to year the equal rights of all members in the common domain, is to ascertain annually the relative value of all tracts (exclusive of improvements) and to collect from each the amount required to equalize all land holdings.

The requirement of permancy of possession, which experience has shown to be beneficent, is secured by perpetual lease, voidable only by the lessee; while the freeing of labor-added values from taxation will encourage every improvement calculated to increase the use-value or add to the enjoyment of the possessor.

The fund thus provided and the taking of which by the community is absolutely necessary to maintain equality of opportunity will be ample for all community purposes, increasing naturally as the needs of the community increase and doing away with all necessity for levy of taxes upon the persons, or labor-created property of others.

Land speculation and monopolization will be effectually destroyed by removing all incentive to the holding of land except for use.

As this system could not be enforced under existing laws against individual land owners the association, as the trustee for all its members, will retain the title to all lands upon which its community is located.

Public Utilities

In the control and operation, by the association, of all "public utilities" the comfort and convenience of the members will be made the first consideration therein, instead of the pecuniary profit of a few investors. Vast sums will be saved to the people, which under the prevailing plan flow into private pockets, and the people of a small community be enabled to enjoy advantages afforded now only by the largest cities, and at much less cost.

The officers of the community will be protected from the corrupting influence exerted by franchise holders seeking to retain or increase their advantages.

Light, power, water (and heat if necessary), will be supplied from the most advantageous point, and will be under one management, and as the land, freed from private speculators, will be so platted as to group the population, without crowding, around a common center, the saving to be effected in these departments can hardly be estimated. It will certainly bring within the command of all those conveniencies [sic]—even necessities—of modern civilization which are now denied entirely to our rural population, and are so expensive that they can be afforded by a very few, comparatively, in the cities.

Insurance of persons and property will also be conducted by the company at the lowest possible cost consistent with absolute safety.

It will be the purpose of the association to supply all these advantages at the earliest practicable moment and the most essential will be furnished as soon as settlement is made upon the chosen site.

Among other things conducive to the comfort, pleasure and elevation of its members which it will be the purpose of the company to provide, as soon as possible, free of charge to individuals, will be public schools, libraries, parks, baths, etc., and to make free speech an actuality, an adequate place of public assemblage, free to all citizens desiring to use, under such regulations only as will secure its proper care and the equal enjoyment thereof by all.

Commercial Features

The commercial advantages to be secured are many and great. A very large part of the cost to the consumer, of almost all commodities, is added after the producer has parted with them, in the complex and antagonistic method of modern exchange. The interests of both producer and consumer demand that the cost of distribution be made as low as possible. If distribution can be so organized that one man can perform the work of two or four without organization, common sense

144

dictates organization. Experience and observation must convince everyone that such a result can be effected by co-operative distribution. The universal approval of government operation of the postal system attests the conviction of all that the efficiency of the service is thus greatly increased and the cost greatly lessened over what it would be with the business in charge of many rival companies. The same reasoning applies with equal force to distributive merchandising.

There are often in a single block a half dozen places for the sale of the same lines of merchandise, occupying a half dozen store rooms, paying rent or taxes thereon, and for light, heat, water, fire and police protection, street paving, cleaning and lighting, insurance, clerks, book-keepers, interest on capital invested in duplicate stocks, etc., where any one of the six with slight increase in space occupied, capital invested and help employed, could serve the trade now divided among all with equal convenience, and, if the saving thus made were divided among the patrons, to their far greater satisfaction. Nor would any hardship be imposed by such a consolidation upon the persons now engaged in such business either as principals or employees. The fierce competition among retail dealers, losses from bad accounts, demoralization or prices by bankrupt stocks thrown on the market at less than ordinary cost to the dealer, and the many other hazards of business, cause a very large percentage of failures in retail trade and keep the survivors filled with anxiety, while for the employees nothing can be expected but a bare living.

By the cheapening of labor products to the consumer, through the great saving effected in co-operative distribution, consumption will be greatly increased and all who are displaced in distribution will be needed in production; while the freeing of the land, the great passive factor in production, will equalize opportunities and enable the employed to secure from the capital investing employer their fair share of the joint product. Producer and consumer will alike be benefited in the greater stability of prices under organized distribution and in the facilities afforded for collecting statistics of relative production and consumption. In its provisions for acting as the agent of its members in the sale of their products outside its limits, our association will apply this rule in dealing directly with the great trade centers of the world's markets, missing the products of many individuals in quantities best suited to the demands of the market, and saving for the producers the share of their product which now goes to local buyers and intermediate brokers in profits, commissions, shortages and the many technical terms which represent the pluckings of middlemen. Other advantages might be shown the chief of which will appear in the discussion of the proposed financial system.

These Rules Do Not Apply To Production

It may appear to some that the rules here laid down in regard to distribution apply to production as well, and that considerations of equal weight demand that the association conduct productive as well as distributive activities, according to the plans of extreme socialists. Careful reflection, however, will, we think, convince anyone that these two great departments of human activity rest on an entirely different basis.

It has been said that competition is war, and all war is destructive, but this is not true. War of individual against individual and nation against nation is destructive, but the conflicts of individuals against the forces of nature are not destructive, but productive. The trade for which men compete in merchandising is practically a fixed quantity. The effects of their strife are shown in the relative shares of that trade gained by each. One thrives at the expense of the other and ofttimes competition, which has been called "the life of trade," proves "the death of traders." It leads to a duplication of efforts in which one is lost. A housewife has a bill of groceries to order, agents of two rival groceries competing for her trade call for her order, one gets it, and the other gets —left, and his efforts are just as much wasted as if he had amused himself by carrying bricks from one pile to another and back again. The same wasteful duplication of effort, though on a more expensive scale, is seen in the contests of rival wholesalers for the trade of retailers.

Competition In Production

brings exactly contrary results. Every motion of an arm or revolution of a wheel is made effective. Human labor and the harnessed forces of nature are utilized to the utmost limit of knowledge. The inventive genius is constantly exercised in devising methods and machinery by which their efficiency may be increased. Under competition production is immensely stimulated, processes cheapened and there is a constant tendency for prices to reach the lowest possible cost of production.

Production differs from distribution, again, in that primarily the individual producer is alone concerned in it. There is a very large part of production in which the producer is also the direct consumer. The farmer and his family consume in large part the fruits and vegetables, the milk and butter, the poultry and eggs, and other products which they produce. It is only the surplus which seeks consumers in the markets, in which the balance of the community is in any wise concerned, and in it their interest and that of the producer is the same, viz: to effect its distribution from one to the other with the greater economy, which can only be done by co-operative distribution as we have shown.

Distribution, however, necessarily involves the interest of more than one individual, and in our complex industrial system generally many, thus logically calling for co-operation to secure mutual benefits.

Leaving production free to individual enterprise furnishes also a scientific solution for the wage problem of those engaged in the public service or in the employ of others, the earnings of like ability and energy in free productive industry being the standard.

Regarding manufacturing enterprises requiring large capital and the labor of many workers, the policy of the association will be to foster voluntary co-operation of both capital and labor investors, but where such enterprises seem vital to the success of the colony, and cannot practicably be secured otherwise, the association may establish and conduct the same as self-supporting departments of its business.

Let it, however, be distinctly borne in mind that, while the association will engage in distributive (and under certain circumstances productive) enterprises it will assume no authority to prohibit any individual member of the community from engaging in any of these enterprises. If any individual should desire to enter into competition with the company's stores he has the undeniable right to do so. If he pays to the community the full rental value of the land he uses he has as much right to establish a grocery upon it and solicit the trade of his fellow citizens as he has to raise potatoes upon it; and other members of the community have the same right to trade with him, if they choose, instead of at the associates stores. In fact, however, it is clear that none would care to enter into competition with the communal system of organized distribution conducted at cost and with the advantages accruing from doing business on a large scale, nor would anyone want to trade away from the company store when it would be impossible for any private store to sell so cheaply.

Financial

A commonly accepted medium of exchange is recognized as a necessity of an advanced civilization. Manifestly it is something which individuals cannot supply each for himself, and which, therefore, it is the duty of the nations to supply in sufficient quantities and on equal terms to their people. The national government under which we live has, however, refused to discharge this plain obligation, but on the contrary, has practically given over to a few non-producers, whose chosen occupation has been recognized by philosophers in all ages as a curse to industry and a menace to liberty, the full control of the financial system of the country, thus making what should be one of the chief aids to the prosperity and advancement of all people, one of the chief instruments for the virtual enslavement of the many by the few.

In its provisions for supplying its members with a safe, adequate and independent medium of exchange will be found one of the most valuable features of our enterprise. We accept the definition of money given by the well known political economist, Francis A. Walker, and approved by the Encyclopedia Britannica: "That which passes freely from hand to hand throughout the community in final discharge of debts and full payment for commodities, being accepted equally without reference to the character or credit of the person who offers it, and without the intention of the person who receives it, to consume it or enjoy it or apply it to any other use than in turn to tender it to others in discharge of debts or payments for commodities."

To supply its members with such a medium our association will issue its non-interest bearing evidences of indebtedness, in whatever form is most convenient and not in conflict with United States statutes, preferably in the form of scrip of the familiar denominations of U. S. currency, which will be put in circulation by paying it out for products offered for sale to or through the association, for advances on non-perishable property stored in the association's warehouses to a safe percentage of its value; for salaries of officers and employees of the association and for services of any kind performed for it.

These evidences of indebtedness the association will receive at their par value in the hands of whomsoever presented, in whatever quantities, for all dues or obligations to the association of whatever nature. As the members of the association will be indebted to it annually for rentals of land occupied by them, and as the association will conduct all public utilities and through its commercial department furnish all staple articles of merchandise, the "redemption" thus provided is full and complete.

148

Some Things The Association Will Not Do

Perhaps the plans of our association will be made more clear by specifying some of the things which it does not propose to do, for it is in these that it differs most from other experiments to found model communities. It does not propose to control ALL the activities of its members; to say what each shall do and what compensation he shall receive for doing it. It does not propose to interfere in any way with the religious beliefs and practices or social intercourse of individuals—to dictate what kind of houses they shall build or what style of clothes they shall wear; to whom they shall sell or of whom they shall buy.

We have here presented the chief features of an association under whose rules we feel confident can be secured advantages which can not be hoped for outside of it or kindred organizations with the lifetime of this generation at least a community wherein he who labors will reap the fruits of his labor, no less, no more; where no robber barons armed with special warrants under the law will bar access to the bounties of nature, or stand on the highways to exact toll from labor caravans; where men instead of wasting their energies in contests where both are sure to lose will join intelligently to make the labor of both most effective; where there will be every incentive to industry and none to idleness; where the necessities of the people will be the concern of all instead of the opportunity of a few; where there will be neither the isolation of the farm nor the crowding of the city; but where the farmer and the worker in store or in factory will enjoy advantages now denied to both; where men, always including women, will be the rulers and wealth the servant. A community, in short, where intelligent men and women, drawn together by a common purpose, will strive to make practical applications of the best thoughts of the best minds of all ages to a solution of the problems which threaten to-day the existence of every nation of the globe. In such an effort we invite the co-operation of all of kindred aims.

> ERNEST B. GASTON
> Des Moines, Iowa, Jan. 15th, 1894.

Appendix Two

Constitution of the Fairhope Industrial Association

PREAMBLE

Believing that the economic conditions under which we now live and labor are unnatural and unjust, in violation of natural rights, at war with the nobler impulses of humanity, and opposed to its highest development; and believing that it is possible by intelligent association, under existing laws, to free ourselves from the greater part of the evils of which we complain, we whose names are hereunto subscribed do associate ourselves together and mutually pledge ourselves to the principles set forth in the following constitution:

Article I. Name

The name of this organization shall be Fairhope Industrial Association.

Article II. Purpose

Its purpose shall be to establish and conduct a model community or colony, free from all forms of private monopoly, and to secure to its members therein, equality of opportunity, the full reward of individual efforts, and the benefits of co-operation in matters of general concern.

Article III. Capital Stock

Sec. 1. The capital stock shall be one million dollars ($1,000,000), divided into five thousand (5,000) shares, of two hundred dollars ($200) each to be paid in under the direction of the executive council.

Sec. 2. Stock shall be transferable only on the books of the association, and to persons acceptable to the association as members.

150

Article IV. Membership

Sec. 1. Any person over eighteen years of age who shall subscribe for at least one share of capital stock, whose application shall be approved by the executive council, shall be a member of the association; provided that ten per cent of the membership may reject any applicant by filing with the secretary their written protest within thirty days after approval of application by the executive council.

Sec. 2. The husband or wife of a member shall, upon signing the constitution, also be considered a member and entitled to a vote in the government of the association, while such relation exists in fact.

Sec. 3. Any member against whom complaint of violation of the spirit and purpose of the association, or invasion of the rights of any of its members is preferred in writing by ten per cent of the membership, may be expelled by the executive council, after full investigation of the charges preferred. Such investigation shall be public and the accused shall be entitled to be represented by counsel.

Sec. 4. In case of expulsion of a member the association shall return to him in lawful money of the United States, the amount contributed by him to the capital stock, and the actual value of any improvement made by him on lands of the association, to be determined by three appraisers, one to be chosen by the trustees, one by the expelled member, and the third by these two.

Article V. Supreme Authority

Sec. 1. Supreme authority shall be vested equally in the membership, to be exercised through the initiative and referendum as hereinafter provided.

Sec. 2. Each member not in arrears to the association shall be entitled to one vote and one only, at all elections.

Article VI. Officers

Sec. 1. The officers of the association shall be: a president; a vice president; a secretary; a treasurer, who shall be superintendent of the department of Finance and Insurance; three trustees; and a superintendent of each of the following departments: Lands and Highways; Public Services; Merchandising; Industries: Public Health.

Sec. 2. The six superintendents of departments shall constitute the executive council of the association.

Sec. 3. The president, vice president, and secretary shall serve for terms of one year. The trustees shall serve for three years, one being elected each year. The superintendents of departments shall serve for terms of two years, the first named being elected on the odd numbered years and the last named three on even numbered years.

Sec. 4. The president shall be the chief executive officer of the association; shall preside over meetings of the executive council and have the deciding vote in case of a tie. He shall countersign all warrants drawn upon the funds of the association under authority of the executive council, and perform such other duties as may herein or hereafter by provided.

Sec. 5. The vice president shall, in case of the death, absence or inability of the president, perform his duties.

Sec. 6. The secretary shall have charge of the records of the association; act as clerk of the executive council; draw and attest all warrants upon the treasurer authorized by the executive council; have charge of the correspondence relating to membership; and prepare annually, and at other times when requested by the board of trustees, full statements of the condition of the association in its various departments.

Sec. 7. The treasurer shall be the custodian of the funds of the association, shall prepare and issue, under direction of the executive council, the association's non-interest bearing obligations hereinafter provided for; and shall have general charge of the financial affairs of the association, including the collection of revenues and the department of insurance. He shall give good and sufficient bond for the faithful accounting of all moneys coming into his hands.

Sec. 8. The trustees shall have general oversight of all affairs of the association; shall have charge of all elections, canvass the votes cast and declare the results thereof; shall act as a committee to audit all accounts and review all reports of officers and employees; and shall annually, and at other times in their discretion, submit reports advising the members fully of the condition and needs of the association's business in all departments. They shall have access to the books and accounts of all officers and all employees at all times. They shall receive compensation only for time actively employed, and shall hold no other office, either by election or appointment.

Sec 9. The superintendents of departments provided for in section two of this article, shall have special supervision of the affairs of the association in their respective departments, and may employ such assistants as they shall deem

152

necessary. They shall present to the executive council annually, and at such other times as requested by it, reports of the condition of the association's business in their departments, and suggest such changes therein as will in their judgment, best promote the interest of the association.

Sec. 10. The executive council shall have general charge of the administration of the affairs of the association, and to that end may make such rules and regulations not inconsistent with its laws as they may deem necessary; may select and employ such agents and assistants not otherwise provided for as they may deem necessary to conduct the association's business; shall fix the compensation of all officers and employees of the association, which compensation shall not, however, exceed the earnings of like ability and energy in productive industry within its limits; shall make an annual appraisal of the rental value of all lands held for lease by the association; and shall perform all other duties necessary to the carrying out of the principles and purposes herein set forth.

Article VII. Initiative and Referendum

Sec. 1. Upon petition of ten per cent of the membership any act of the executive council, legislative or administrative, or any measure set forth in said petition, shall be submitted to a vote of the membership.

Sec. 2. No measure of general legislation passed by the executive council shall be in force until thirty days have elapsed after its passage without the filing of a petition for its submission to the membership; provided, that nothing in this section shall be construed to prevent the immediate taking effect of any order of the executive council necessary to the execution of the measures already in force.

Sec. 3. Upon petition of twenty per cent of the membership the question of the dismissal of any officer, however elected or appointed, must be submitted to a popular vote.

Article VIII. Elections

Sec. 1. The regular annual election shall be held on the first Thursday of February of each year.

Sec. 2. Special elections may be held at any time, at the discretion of the executive council, or on petition of ten per cent of the membership, after thirty days notice.

Sec. 3. At all elections printed official ballots shall be prepared, under the direction of the board of trustees, on which shall appear in full any measure to be voted upon, and the names of all candidates who may be placed in nomination in manner hereinafter provided.

Sec. 4. Nominations for office may be made by petition of five per cent of the membership filed with the secretary ten days before election.

Sec. 5. The name of any officer whose term of office expires at any election shall appear on the official ballot as a candidate for re-election unless he shall have become disqualified to fill the position, or his declination in writing be filed with the secretary ten days before said election.

Sec. 6. All voting shall be by secret ballot.

Sec. 7. The affirmative votes of three-fourths of the members shall be necessary to amend or repeal any part of this constitution.

Sec. 8. In the election of officers or on the passage of any measure not conflicting with this constitution, the decision of a majority of those voting shall be final.

Sec. 9. Should no candidate for any office receive a majority of the votes cast at any election the trustees shall order a second election to be held two weeks thereafter for such officer, but only the names of the three candidates receiving the highest number of votes shall appear on the official ballot at said second election. If at the second election no candidate receives a majority, a third election shall be held two weeks thereafter, but only the two names receiving the highest number of votes at said election shall appear on the official ballot.

Article IX. Land

Sec. 1. There shall be no individual ownership of land within the jurisdiction of the association, but the association shall hold as trustee for its entire membership, the title to all lands upon which its community shall be maintained.

Sec. 2. Its lands shall be equitably divided and leased to members at an annually appraised rental which shall equalize the varying advantages of location and natural qualities of different tracts, and convert into the treasury of the association for the common benefit of all of its members, all values attaching to such lands not arising from the efforts and expenditures thereon of the lessees.

Sec. 3. Land leases shall convey full and absolute right to the use and control of lands so leased, and to the ownership and disposition of all improvements made or products produced thereon so long as the lessee shall pay the annually appraised rentals provided in the foregoing section, and may be terminated by the lessee after six months' notice in writing to the association and the payment of all rents due

154

thereon.

Sec. 4. Leaseholds may be assignable but only to members of the association. Such assignments must be filed for record in the office of the secretary and the person to whom the same is assigned thereby becomes the tenant of the association.

Sec. 5. The association shall have a prior lien on all property held by any lessee upon lands of the association, for all arrearages of rent.

Sec. 6. If any lessee shall exact or attempt to exact from another a greater value for the use of land, exclusive of improvements, than the rent paid by him to the association, the executive council shall, immediately on proof of such fact, increase the rental charge against such land to the amount so charged or sought to be charged.

Sec. 7. Nothing shall be construed to invalidate the association's right of eminent domain. In all leases of lands the association shall reserve the right to resume the possession of the same for public purposes, on payment of all damages sustained by the lessee thereby, to be determined by three appraisers, one to be chosen by the board of trustees, one by the lessee and the third by these two.

Article X. Financial

Sec. 1. To provide its members with a safe, adequate, and independent medium for effecting exchanges of property and services, the association may issue its non-interest bearing obligations, which shall be receivable by it at face value in full payment of all its demands.

Sec. 2. These obligations may be issued for the purchase and handling of all merchandise; for advances on goods stored in the association's warehouses to a safe percentage of their values; and for all expenses of the public services; but no more shall be issued for such public service during any year than the estimated revenue available during said year for such purpose.

Article XI. Public Utilities

No private franchise for the supplying of its members with such public necessities as water, light, heat, power, transportation facilities, irrigating systems, etc., shall ever be granted by the association, but it shall as soon as practicable, erect and maintain the necessary plants, and perform such services, converting all revenues therefrom into the general treasury of the association.

Article XII. Distribution and Production

Sec. 1. To effect in distribution the efficiency and economy demanded in the interests alike of producers and consumers, the association shall establish a store or stores at which shall be kept for sale all articles of merchandise for which there shall be sufficient demand.

Sec. 2. Such merchandise shall be sold to members and non-members alike, at prices approximately those prevailing in the locality where the association's community may be located, and from the profits arising therefrom, the executive council may at its discretion set aside a portion to be paid into the general treasury of the association and a portion to be used as additional capital in said stores. The remainder shall be divided among the members trading at said stores, in proportion to their other purchases.

Sec. 3. For the purpose of accumulating capital with which to purchase stock for such stores the executive council may at its discretion require of each member before taking residence upon its lands the payment of a sum not to exceed one hundred dollars for which shall be issued its non-interest bearing obligations described in article ten.

Sec. 4. A department shall also be established to assist the association's members in the disposition of their surplus products to the greatest advantage. To this end staple products may be purchased at the market price by the management, or handled on commission as desired. Convenient and safe storage shall also be provided.

Sec. 5. Believing that the free competition of free men in productive industry is natural and beneficent, and that therefrom will arise a natural and just co-operation in enterprises requiring the associated labor and capital of individuals, it is the declared general policy of this association to leave production free to individual enterprise. It reserves the right, however, to establish and conduct manufactories and industries of any kind.

Sec. 6. Nothing in this article shall be construed to give the association the authority to establish a monopoly in any of the departments herein mentioned; and the same shall be maintained on a self-supporting basis, so far as possible.

Article XIII. Insurance

Recognizing insurance as a proper department of public business the association will provide for the insurance of its members and their property when desired, at approximate cost of the service.

Article XIV. Parks, Libraries, Etc.

Ample provision shall be made in platting the lands of the association for land for parks and all other public purposes; and as rapidly as may be, lands thus intended shall be improved and beautified; and schools, libraries, public halls, natatoriums, etc., established and maintained at the expense of the association for the free use and enjoyment of the members and their families.

Article XV. No Taxation

No taxes or charges of any kind other than hereinbefore provided for shall be levied by the association upon the property or persons of its members.

Article XVI. Payment of Taxes

All taxes levied by the state, county or township on the property of the association or any of its members held within its jurisdiction, credits excepted, shall be paid out of the general fund of the association.

Article XVII. May deal with Non-Members

Lands not desired for use by members may be leased to non-members, and any services which the association may undertake to perform for its members may be performed also for non-members, at the discretion of the executive council, on such terms as it may provide.

Article XVIII. Individual Freedom

The natural rights of its members to absolute freedom in production, exchange, association, beliefs, and worship shall never be abrogated or impaired by the association, and the only limit to the exercise of the will of individuals shall be the equal rights of all others.

Index

161